DOODLE SCHOOL

A Daily Design Challenge to Up Your Free-Motion Quilting Game

Dara Tomasson and Amy Colleen Robertson

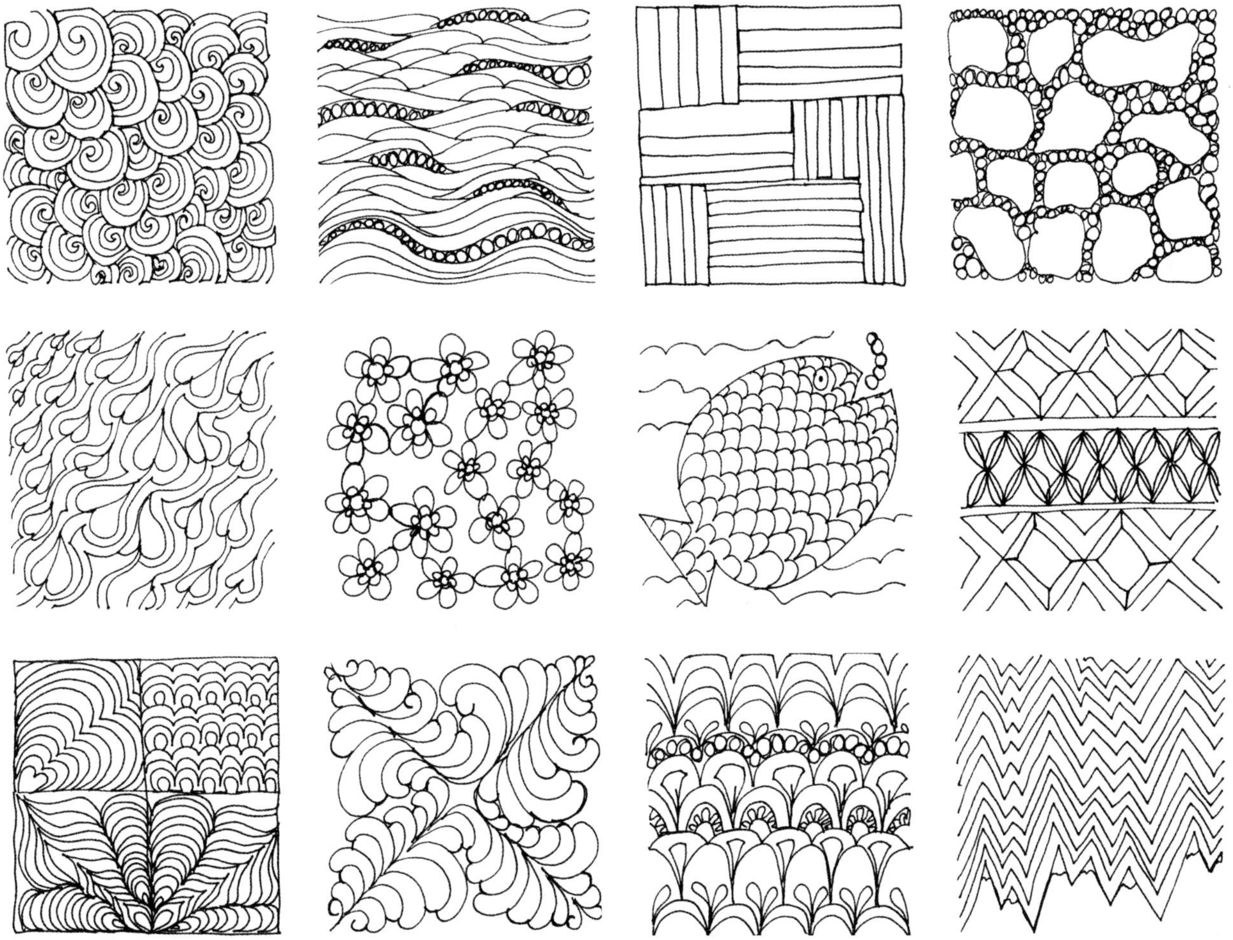

stashBOOKS®
an imprint of C&T Publishing

PUBLISHER: Amy Barrett-Daffin

CREATIVE DIRECTOR: Gailen Runge

ACQUISITIONS EDITOR: Roxane Cerda

MANAGING EDITOR: Liz Aneloski

EDITOR: Beth Baumgartel

TECHNICAL EDITOR: Susan Allen

COVER/BOOK DESIGNER: April Mostek

PRODUCTION COORDINATOR: Zinnia Heinzmann

PRODUCTION EDITOR: Alice Mace Nakanishi

ILLUSTRATORS: Dara Tomasson, Amy Colleen Robertson, and Mary E. Flynn

PHOTOGRAPHY: *As listed here, unless otherwise noted*

Front cover: Vanessa Lust

Front and back cover details, Dedication/Acknowledgments, Contents, and page 124: Estefany Gonzalez of C&T Publishing, Inc.

Page 6: Vanessa Lust

Page 9: Amy Colleen Robertson

Page 10: Vanessa Lust

Photography on the following pages provided by Shutterstock.com:

Page 12: Pixeljoy (*left*); finchfocus (*right*); johnfoto18 (*bottom*)

Page 15: Nik Merkulov (*top right*); Tim UR (*bottom left*); Rudmer Zwerver (*bottom right*)

Page 18: Yarygin (*left*); Alexander_DG (*top right*); Ron Dale (*bottom right*)

Page 22: COLOA Studio (*left*); Yamelahz (*top right*); Christine C Brooks (*bottom right*)

Page 26: Alexapicso (*top left*); Billion Photos (*bottom left*); Peter Zijlstra (*bottom right*)

Page 29: Africa Studio (*top left*); Rawpixel.com (*bottom left*); banjongseal324 (*right*)

Page 32: Aptyp_koK (*left*); Barnabas Davoti (*top right*); dimid_86 (*bottom right*)

Page 36: Stor24 (*top*); Photos BrianScantlebury (*bottom left*); Ratchanee Sawasdijira (*bottom right*)

Page 39: ClareM (*left*); nine_far (*top right*); Francisco Javier Diaz (*bottom right*)

Page 42: paristochina (*top left*); Freer (*bottom left*); Liderina (*bottom right*)

Page 45: Sabphoto (*top left*); Andrey tiyk (*top right*); Evgeny Bakharev (*bottom*)

Page 49: Roman Chazov (*top left*); NivCube (*bottom left*); KAY4YK (*right*)

Page 52: r.classen (*top left*); charles taylor (*bottom left*); VLADJ55 (*right*)

Page 56: Parinya Feungchan (*top left*); Billion Photos (*top right*); Opalfrost (*bottom*)

Page 59: Photos BrianScantlebury (*left*); Pixel-Shot (*top right*); Jerry Lin (*bottom right*)

Page 62: Andrew Hagen (*left*); Scisetti Alfio (*top right*); M. Kropp (*bottom right*)

Page 66: mycteria (*left*); Chursina Viktoriia (*top right*); Naomi Hasegawa (*bottom right*)

Page 70: BurAnd (*top left*); Sanit Fuangnakhon (*bottom left*); K.Kargona (*right*)

Page 74: Master1305 (*left*); Tatiana Bobkova (*top right*); Lamyai (*bottom right*)

Page 78: NavinTar (*left*); pattanapong keawudon (*top right*); Tala-Natali (*bottom right*)

Page 82: Tymonko Galyna (*top*); EpicStockMedia (*bottom left*); LedyX (*bottom right*)

Page 86: Naphat_Jorjee (*top left*); Hi-Point (*top right*); mrfiza (*bottom*)

Page 90: EVGEIIA (*top left*); VarnaK (*bottom left*); Anatoli Styf (*right*)

Page 94: OlScher (*top left*); Praew stock (*top right*); Bildagentur Zoonar GmbH (*bottom*)

Page 98: fewerton (*top left*); Dan Thornberg (*bottom left*); Raywoo (*right*)

Page 101: Good luck images (*top left*); Scorpp (*top right*); Dimitrios P (*bottom*)

Page 105: Anton Petrus (*left*); Nataliia Antonova (*top right*); fanjianhua (*bottom right*)

Page 109: Milles Studio (*left*); vlastas (*top right*); yurakrasil (*bottom right*)

Page 113: Trompinex (*top left*); Luca Lorenzelli (*bottom left*); Svet_Feo (*right*)

Page 117: SGuillory (*top left*); photo.ua (*bottom left*); WitthayaP (*right*)

Page 121: Vadym Lesyk (*top left*); Sinisa Botas (*bottom left*); Vaclav Volrab (*right*)

Published by Stash Books, an imprint of C&T Publishing, Inc., P.O. Box 1456, Lafayette, CA 94549

Library of Congress Cataloging-in-Publication Data

Names: Tomasson, Dara, 1973- author. | Robertson, Amy Colleen, 1972- author.

Title: Doodle school : a daily design challenge to up your free-motion quilting game / Dara Tomasson and Amy Colleen Robertson.

Description: Lafayette : Stash Books, an imprint of C&T Publishing, [2021]

Identifiers: LCCN 2021008443 | ISBN 9781644030905 (trade paperback) | ISBN 9781644030912 (ebook)

Subjects: LCSH: Machine quilting--Patterns.

Classification: LCC TT835 .T6429 2021 | DDC 746.46--dc23

LC record available at https://lccn.loc.gov/2021008443

Printed in the USA

10 9 8 7 6 5 4 3 2 1

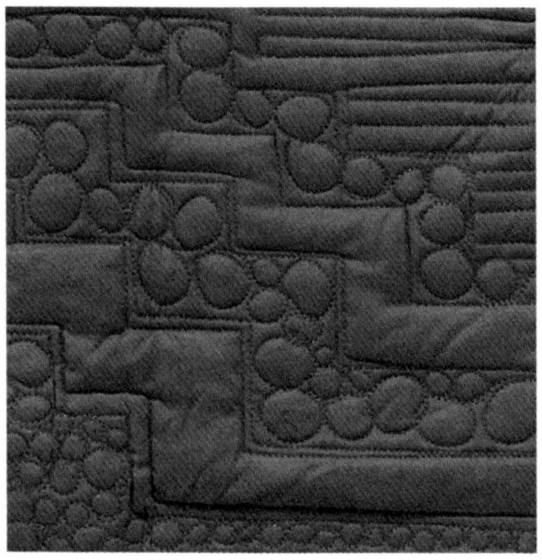

Dedication

To my four sons and daughter for teaching me patience, love, and how to be more Christlike. To my husband for being my best friend, my biggest supporter, and the love of my life. ***Dara***

To my mother, Carin Snyder, who has a head full of horse stories that have never been published. Thank you for believing in me and loving me unconditionally and for sharing so many of your talents. ***Amy***

Acknowledgments

So grateful for Amy, who jumped in with both feet to create this book with me. I also want to thank Deena Rutter for inspiring me to really dream bigger than I ever imagined by teaching me the tools that have literally changed my life beyond everything I thought was possible. ***Dara***

Thank you, Dara, for inviting me to create this book with you. It has been an honor and an incredible opportunity. Thanks to my husband, Tim, and my kids for their patience when I was completely unavailable during the final days before my first deadlines. Thank you to everyone at Nuttall's and the long list of teachers, in person and online, who have trained me in longarm quilting. Thank you to my fabulous customers who trust me with their precious quilts. Finally, thank you to Beth, Roxane, Liz, Susan, Zinnia, and everyone at C&T Publishing / Stash Books for bringing this book into the world. ***Amy***

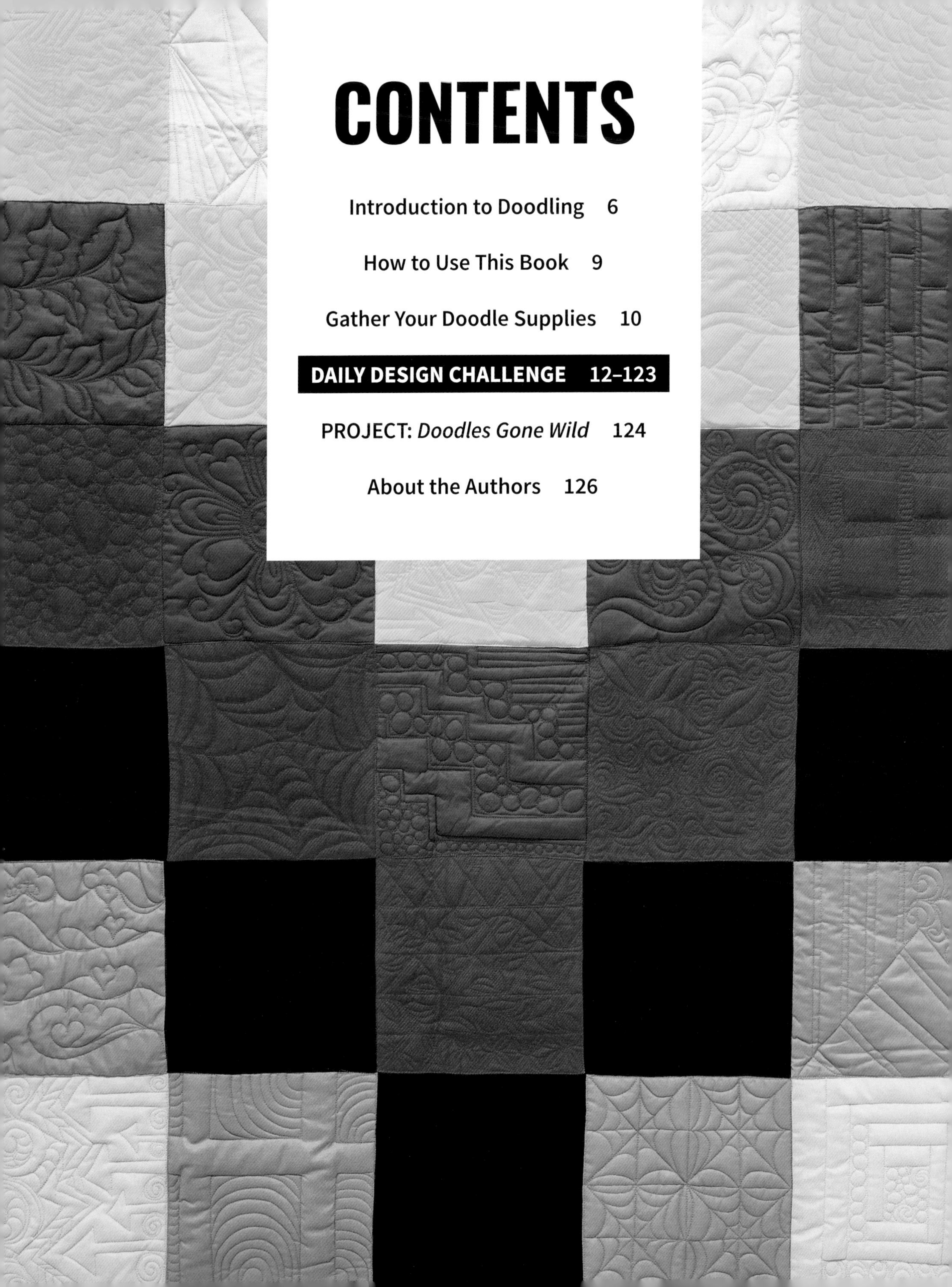

CONTENTS

DAILY DESIGN CHALLENGE

12

Day 1: Lines

15
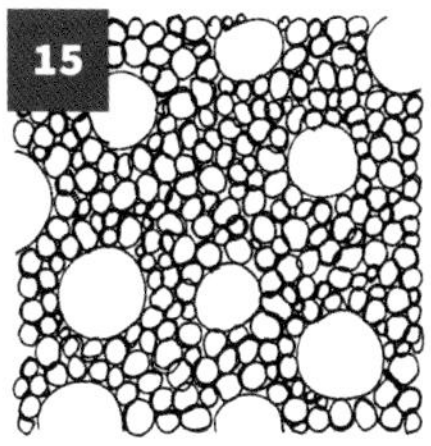
Day 2: Circles

18

Day 3: Swirls

22

Day 4: Leaves

26
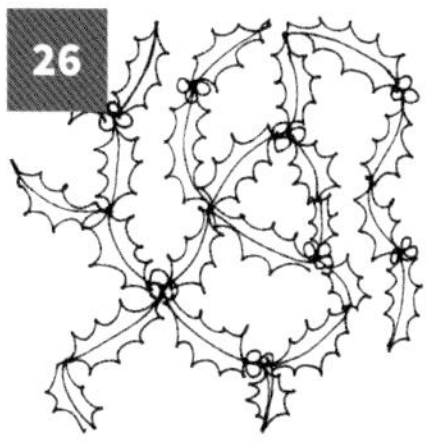
Day 5: Holly

29

Day 6: Bubbles

32
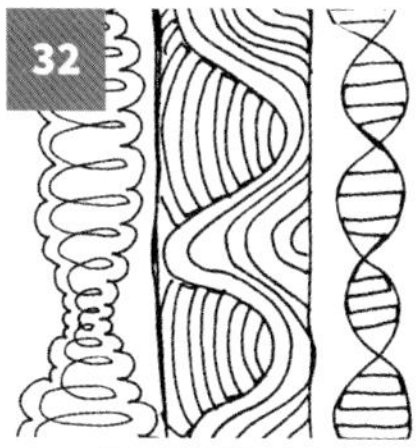
Day 7: Twist

36
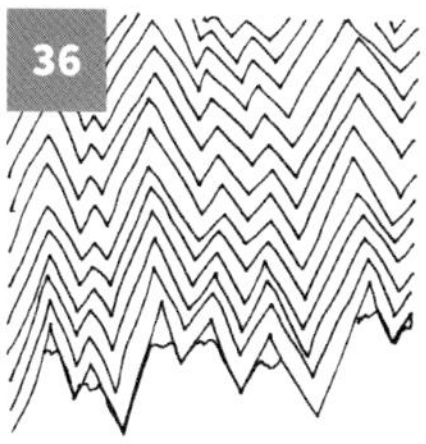
Day 8: Echoes

39
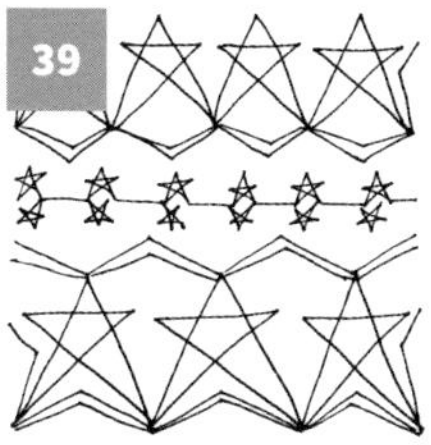
Day 9: Stars

42

Day 10: Triangles

45

Day 11: Clouds

49

Day 12: Hearts

52
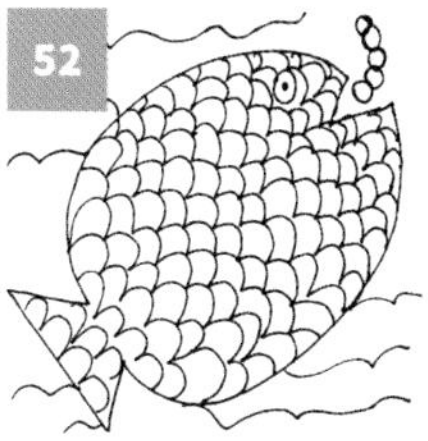
Day 13: Scale

56
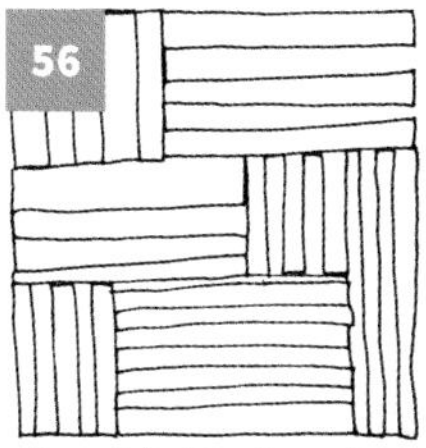
Day 14: Rectangles

59
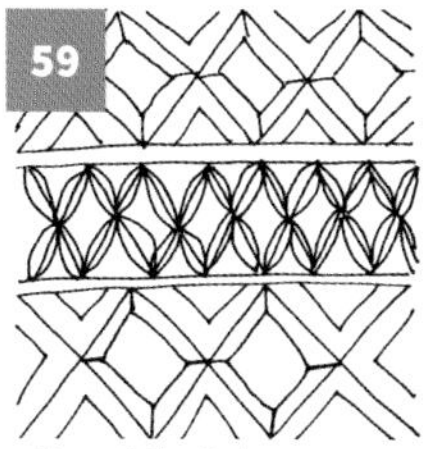
Day 15: Crisscross

62

Day 16: Vines

66

Day 17: Feathers

70

Day 18: Clamshells

74
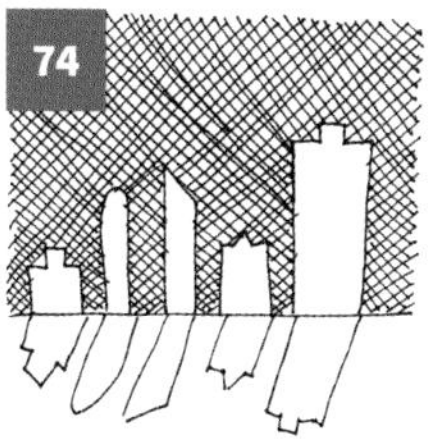
Day 19: Shadows

78

Day 20: Walls

82
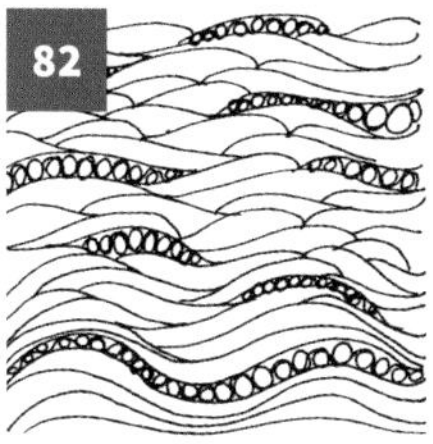
Day 21: Water

86

Day 22: Repeat

90
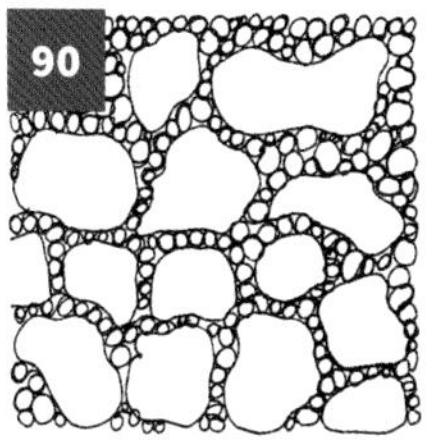
Day 23: Rocks and Pebbles

94
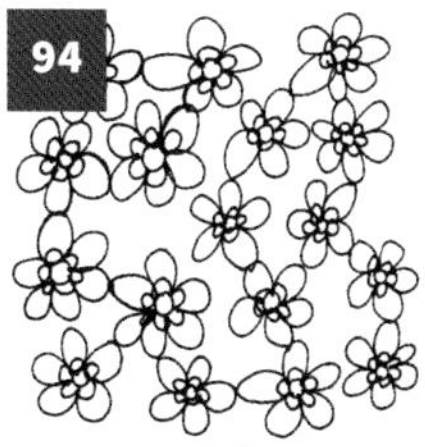
Day 24: Flowers

98

Day 25: Arrows

101

Day 26: Shells

105

Day 27: Windows

109
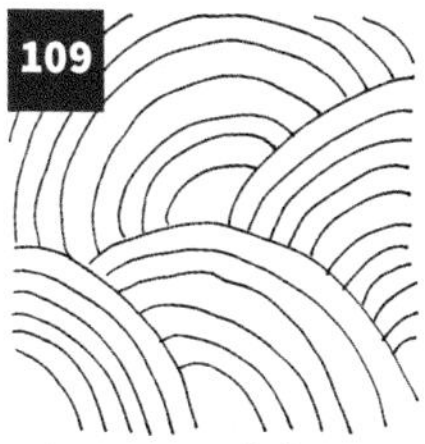
Day 28: Rainbows

113

Day 29: Zigzags

117

Day 30: Borders

121

Day 31: Spider Webs

INTRODUCTION TO DOODLING

Welcome to Doodle School! We're so excited you've decided to join us. Doodling is one of the best ways to boost your free-motion quilting confidence and jumpstart your free-motion skills. How do we know? Because we're both continuous-line doodlers. We've seen the difference doodling has made in our free-motion quilting.

What do we mean when we say we're "continuous-line" doodlers? When we doodle for free-motion practice, we draw our entire doodle without lifting our pens from the paper. This is important because when you are free-motion quilting, you nearly always create your designs with a continuous line of stitching. If you want to truly simulate the experience of free-motion quilting when you doodle, you've got to doodle with a continuous line.

Why Doodle?

You may be wondering, "Why doodle? Why not just practice free-motion quilting on my machine?" There are so many great reasons to doodle. That's why we're so enthusiastic about it.

Doodle to Save Money

Let's start with cost savings. Doodling on paper is much less expensive than practicing on your machine. When you practice on your machine, you use thread, fabric, and batting every time. You also use your machine, which means more wear and tear on your most expensive quilting tool.

You also run the risk of ruining precious quilt tops if you decide to quilt them before you've had some practice. Even seasoned quilters doodle out ideas before they start quilting on the machine.

Experienced quilters also want to know how their design will look before they start stitching. It makes sense, doesn't it? Haven't we all had experience with envisioning things a certain way in our heads only to find that they don't look nearly as good in reality? When in doubt, doodle it out. In fact, doodle it out even if you are certain.

Doodle to Save Yourself Stress

Traveling around the quilt, entering and exiting designs, and traveling within a design are all things that can be quite stressful if you haven't thought them out before you started quilting. Doodling your designs beforehand takes so much of this stress away.

Doodle for Convenience

You can't take your machine with you when you pick your kids up from school. While you're waiting in the car, however, you can always pull out your notebook and get some doodling practice. And what about doodling before bed? We'd like to see you take your machine to bed with you!

Doodle to Get Inspired

Doodling also gives you more opportunity to experiment and be creative. You can play as much as you like in your notebook. If something doesn't work out, well, it's not a big loss. What you'll find, however, is that when you play with your doodles, you come up with ideas that surprise you. When you're quilting, you usually don't want to take risks. But if you're not taking risks, you're also not going to try anything new. Taking risks and discovering new designs is so much easier when you doodle.

Doodle to Keep a Record

Another wonderful thing about doodles is that they're easy to save. Doodles fit neatly into your notebooks, on thin sheets of paper. They are much easier to save than quilt sandwiches! Why should you save your doodles? You might be surprised if we told you how many times we've referred back to our doodles for ideas and inspiration. Even the doodles that didn't look very good when we drew them have sparked new ideas when we've looked at them later. Any doodle can be a great jumping-off point for a new idea.

While you're doodling, use that as a time to take notes. Write down things that come to mind that you don't want to forget. Circle areas in your doodles that you want to improve. Scribble in the margins or anywhere you find a space. This way, your doodle journal becomes a place where you can observe and reflect.

Doodle to Decide

Doodling helps you see what a design will look like on a quilt. Another advantage of doodling is that you can try out multiple plans for a quilt. You can draft out your quilt, make some copies, and try a few different quilting plans. Doodling a few designs on paper provides the opportunity to compare and contrast ideas.

Doodle to Increase Your Skills

Doodling is also a wonderful way to build muscle memory. When you practice designs repeatedly, your body and your mind work together so that you can quilt your designs nearly effortlessly. Your curves become smoother and your lines straighter. Your aim becomes nearly perfect. Time spent doodling increases your confidence when you bring your designs to the machine.

Doodle to Save Your Body

Doodling your designs over and over (with breaks, might we mention) puts much less strain on your body than quilting them over and over. We won't lie, you probably will experience some hand cramping when you doodle. The right types of pens tend to lessen cramping (see Pens, page 10).

Doodle to See Your Progress

We've already talked about doodling as a convenient way to keep a record. One reason you might want to keep a record is so that you can see how far you've come. Sometime in the future, you may feel like you're not getting anywhere. We all hit walls and we all get discouraged sometimes. Your doodle notebooks can be a wonderful remedy for discouragement. When you look through your doodles, recognize your hard work and give yourself the praise you deserve.

Doodle to Celebrate!

Months and then years from now, when you pull out one of your well-worn doodle notebooks, look at your progress and use that as an excuse to celebrate! Celebrate the wonderful free-motion quilter you've become. Celebrate the diligence you've shown. Celebrate the knowledge you've gained. Celebrate that you've spent time in the creative process. Just celebrate! We all need more reasons to celebrate.

HOW TO USE THIS BOOK

Each of the 31 doodle chapters features the following sections to provide inspiration, technical assistance, directions on how to doodle specific designs, and a few coaching tips!

Prompt

Each day starts with a prompt. Read the prompt and the accompanying introduction. Take a few minutes to brainstorm ideas, write your ideas in your doodle book, and search online or in books for more inspiration (including designs other free-motion quilters have shared). The free-motion quilting community is very generous about sharing what they've learned.

Photos

After each introductory prompt, we've included photographs from everyday life to inspire you!

Technical Assistance

This is where we provide guidance for forming the basic shapes and designs for the prompt. We've spent years perfecting these designs and we want to share our technical knowledge so that, if your designs just aren't coming out right, you will know how to improve them.

Applications

We'll walk you through some designs that use the day's prompt. Most of the designs are simple; a few are more complicated. We try to start simple so that you can build your skills gradually. There are a few more advanced designs that we love so much that we just couldn't help sharing them. Try them if you feel comfortable with it. If you don't feel ready, they'll still be here when you are ready.

Coaching

In this section, we encourage you and give you the information you need to be successful. Dara is a successful life coach who helps clients reach their goals every day. She is also Amy's coach. Together they generously share many valuable skills for life, doodling, and free-motion quilting.

Final Project

A fabulous quilt project, *Doodles Gone Wild* (page 124), will help you transition from doodling to free-motion quilting. This project is your opportunity to take the doodles you've learned about and created on paper and use them to make your own quilt. Because the focus of this book is about doodling, we refer you to Dara's book *Walk, Jog, Run—A Free-Motion Quilting Workout* (page 126), for help getting started and/or learning more about free-motion quilting.

NOTE *For more details and videos about the Daily Design Challenges, go to YouTube and search Dara Tomasson Doodle Challenge.*

GATHER YOUR DOODLING SUPPLIES

The correct tools make everything easier for doodling and for quilting.

Pens

Two good pen choices for doodling are ink and felt-tip pens. Practice with a variety of pens to determine which type allows you to write smoothly and with very little pressure. The better the ink flow, the less likely your hands will cramp.

A fine-tip Crayola marker, for example, is a great tool for practice, but the tip is not fine enough for the detail work. Ink pens come in a variety of sizes; the sizes indicate the width of the lines the pens make. A 0.5mm pen creates a line that is 0.5mm wide.

TIP Dara used to love 0.5mm pens, but now that she has experimented, she feels that 0.7mm pens allow better ink flow without compromising the detail work of the design.

Paper

There are all different grades of paper available. We prefer a smooth paper that is not too thick. If your paper is too thick, your pen can sink down and dig into it. A thin, firm paper minimizes the pressure on your hand and wrist and results in less fatigue.

Whiteboards

Drawing on a whiteboard is a good idea because the surface is so smooth. The pen glides easily which reduces fatigue. Just take care not to smudge your marker with the heel of your hand. If you use a whiteboard, make sure you take a picture of your doodles or copy them into your notebook before you wipe them away.

Notebooks

Designate a notebook or journal to use only for your doodles. It should have blank white paper, with no lines. You can find wonderful and inexpensive notebooks at the dollar store.

You want a notebook that you can carry with you so that you can practice doodling during those found moments in your day. Your notebook should be durable and easy to use with paper heavy enough to prevent ink from bleeding through the pages.

Here are a few considerations when purchasing a notebook:

SIZE: Does it fit in your purse? Will you want to carry this doodle book around with you?

PAPER THICKNESS: Thick paper and a thin pen can cause a tired hand because of the amount of pressure you must apply for drawing. To reduce hand cramping, we recommend this rule of thumb: Thicker paper requires a larger tip on the pen.

TYPE OF PAPER: Is it smooth? Will it be slippery? Will your favorite pen write on it easily? Will the ink smear?

BINDING: While coil-bound notebooks might have some advantages, we find that the pages tend to rip out and the notebook doesn't last as long.

TIP Dara buys packing paper from U-Haul to practice new designs. She sketches out the block or a portion of a quilt and practices drawing. Not only does this help her see if she likes what she has created, but she also establishes the flow for the design so that she has fewer stops and starts.

NOTE Share Your Doodles

We would love to see the fabulous doodles you create. As you progress through this book, be sure to take photos of your doodles and post them to Instagram and Facebook with the hashtag ***#freemotiondoodleschool****. Be sure to tag us in your posts (see our social media tags, pages 126 and 127). We can't wait to see your work!*

We will be hosting online doodle challenges regularly. Be sure to follow us on Instagram and Facebook so that we can make sure you don't miss them. The challenges are a great way to build your skills, meet other free-motion quilters, and share your work. We hope you'll join us.

DAY 1: LINES

Prompt

We're starting with a straight line—the most basic, simplest mark.

Why is it that, for many of us, the act of drawing a straight line can seem so daunting? Don't worry, there's a simple fix for that: a ruler. (It's not cheating. We promise.) Think of a ruler as a tool. It can help you get past the hurdle of putting that first mark down on your page.

So, if you're concerned about how your lines are going to turn out, don't be! They really don't need to be perfect. But if you want nice, straight lines, just grab a ruler or maybe a note card with a straight edge and start doodling.

Technical Assistance

Start by thinking about the distance between your lines. You can space them equally apart, like piano keys. Equally spaced lines create an even texture and a precise, clean look in a quilt. On the other hand, you can use random spacing between your lines, such as what you would see in a bar code. Irregularly spaced lines seem to have a more frantic movement—almost like bees buzzing around a garden. The spacing between your lines can affect the mood and the message in your design.

Also, think about the directions of your lines. They can be horizontal, vertical, or diagonal. Do you want any angles in your lines? Do you want any of your lines to intersect? All these choices also affect the overall mood of your design, whether it's in a doodle or a quilt. Play around with angles and spaces until you arrive at something that fits the mood you want to create.

Applications

1 GREEK KEY: Concentrate on doubling the space between your lines as you go into the key so you have the space you will need to turn around and exit the key. Be sure to leave space under the key so that you can get to your next destination.

---

2 STEPPING UP: Repetition is a classic technique with endless possibilities. Create any type of line and repeat it.

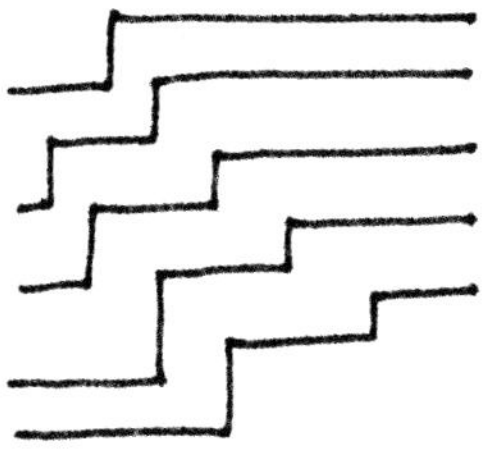

---

3 STRIPS: Draw paths and then fill the spaces between them with designs of your choice.

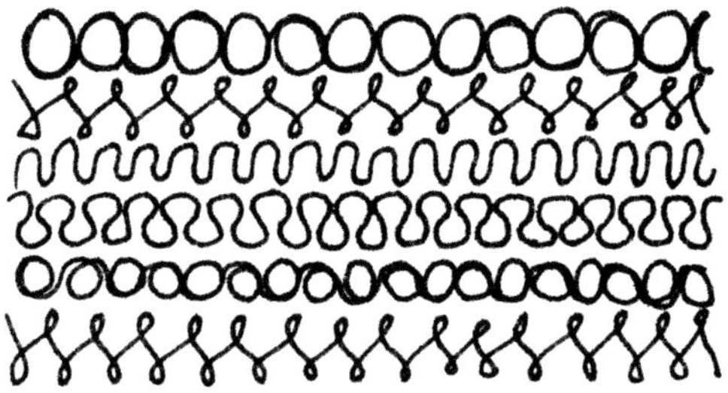

4 **RANDOM:** Our brains like symmetry but they're intrigued by asymmetry; use either to create the doodle you desire.

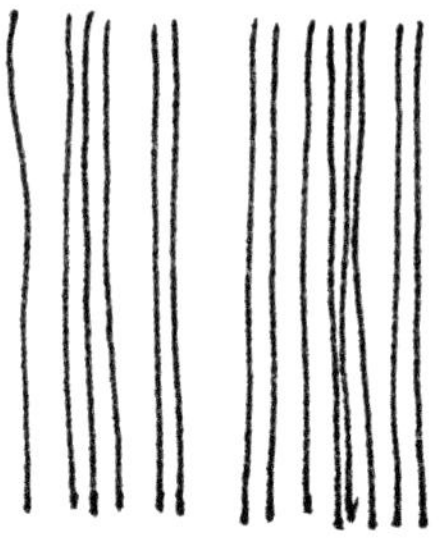

5 **CRISSCROSS/PLAID:** Draw parallel lines in one direction. Then draw lines in the opposite direction, crossing over your original lines. Space your lines evenly to create a grid. Alternate the spacing between your lines to create a plaid effect.

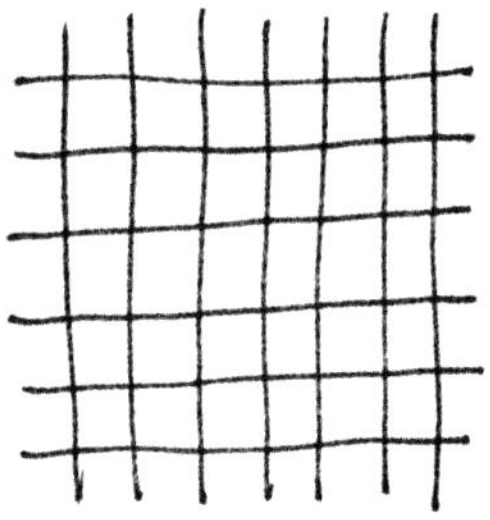

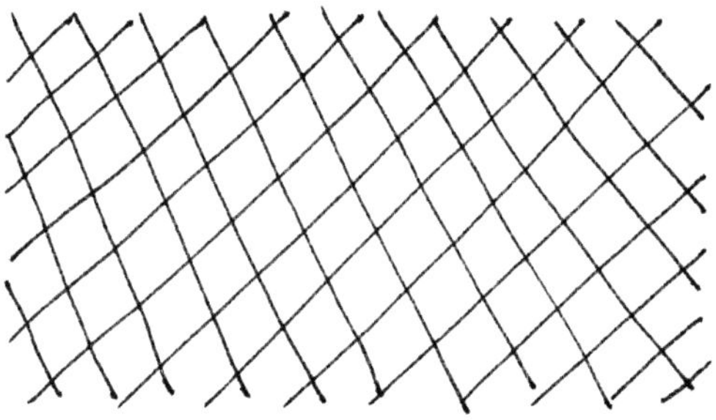

Coaching

What Is Your Purpose of Learning?

If you know why you want to participate in the Doodle School, you are much more likely to complete all 31 days and get the full benefit from your effort. We want to help you clarify your purpose right from the start. Take a few minutes and think about your reasons for joining the challenge. Do you want to improve your skills? Perhaps you want to finish partially completed quilts. Maybe you want to start using your free-motion quilting to earn some extra spending money. Do you want to quilt for a charity or make a stockpile of quilts to gift? There are many reasons to rise to the challenge—figure out yours and join us.

DAY 2: CIRCLES

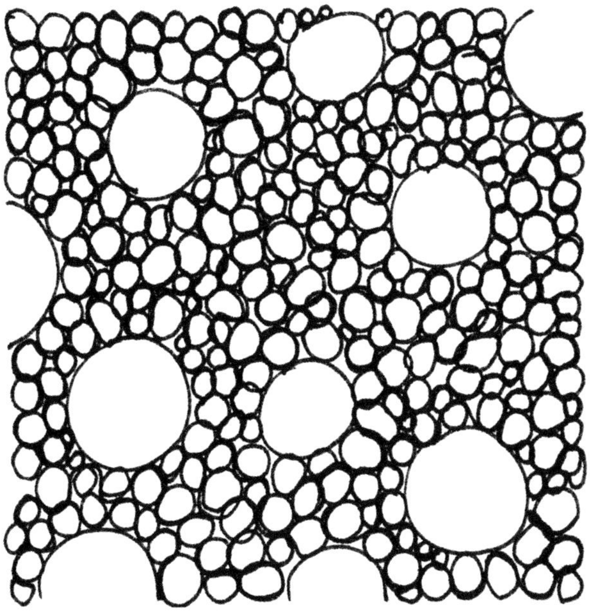

Prompt

What are the first images that come to mind with this design prompt?

Write them down. When your brain associates the circle design with real life objects you can recreate them with greater ease.

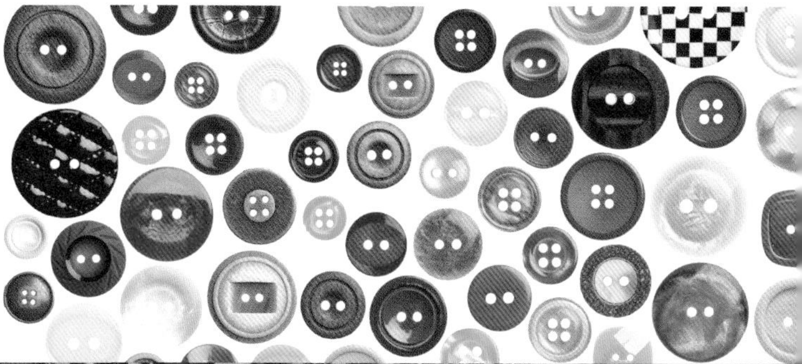

Technical Assistance

There is a technique to creating beautiful circles when free-motion quilting. It is important to complete the first circle before creating the following circles. When we quilt circles, we pause for a split second when the circle is complete. By assuring that the circle is one complete line, the circle maintains its shape. If the circle is rushed, for example, it can tend to look more like scribbles or ovals.

Think about how circles can fit together: Pebbles on a beach randomly fit together with all their different sizes, yet a string of pearls line up side by side.

Applications

1 **GRIDDED CIRCLES:** In this example, we created side-by-side circles using a grid for consistent sizing. The grid helps you draw them all the same size.

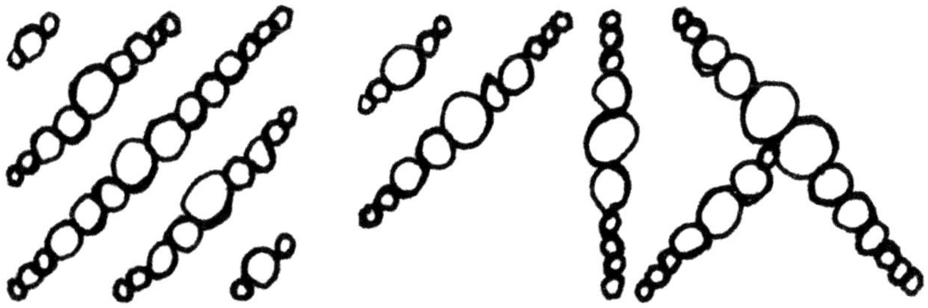

2 **PEARL NECKLACE:** Just like a pearl necklace that graduates in size from small to large to small again, this design copies that format. To recreate this design, you need to design a plan and then follow it. Perhaps drawing some faint lines for where the circles are going to go would be helpful. We like to "finger draw" where we are going to go before putting pencil to paper. Finger drawing is such a useful, transferable skill when free-motion quilting with fabric.

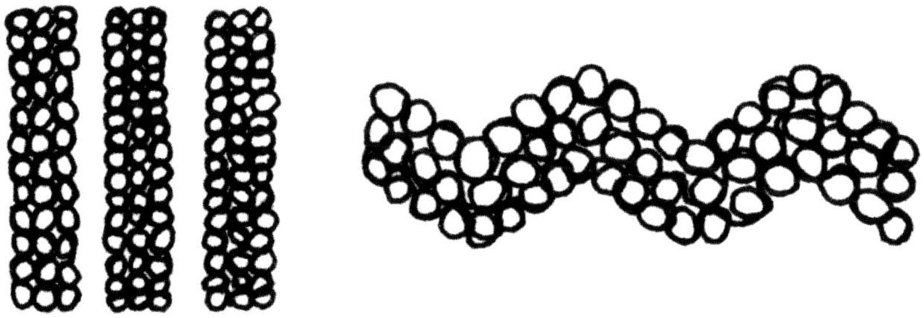

3 **CIRCLE CLUSTERS:** This example solidifies the importance of closing the circles because the circles are so small that if they aren't closed, they look more like scribbles. Another great benefit to practicing with this design is that it's also linear. We like to keep the direction simple. Learning how to free-motion quilt takes up a lot of concentration (Dara calls it "mind juice"). When the direction is simple you don't have to worry about where to go and can just focus on the shapes!

4 **ALLOVER CIRCLES:** In Canada, Dara uses different-size coins for circle inspiration: nickels, dimes, quarters, loonies, and twonies. So, imagine all the coins laying out on the counter. To free-motion quilt all these different-size coins, think about them nestling together and fitting into each other. One of the ways to assure this happens is to "talk to yourself" by saying loonie, penny, nickel, dime. Or small, medium and large. It is important to practice saying the different shapes while doodling them.

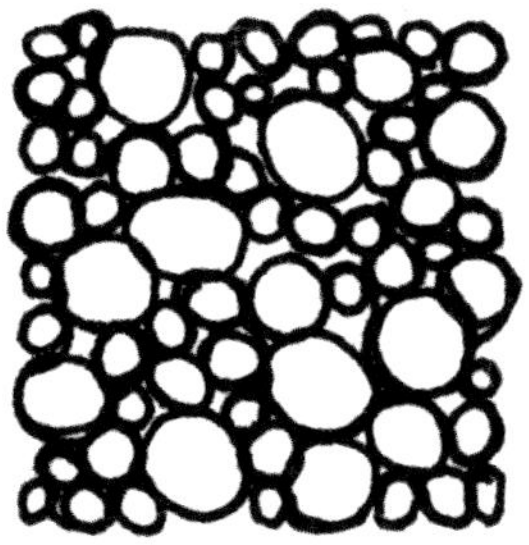

---

5 **ABACUS:** Using linear quilting is super helpful because it gives direction on which way to go. The abacus design can be created vertically, horizontally, or diagonally. The spacing between lines can also be varied. When drawing this design, be mindful of the size of circles that you wish to create. The look of the design can be altered dramatically by playing around with various sizes of circles. We encourage you to experiment. One technical element to keep in mind is to trace back carefully on the circle line. We suggest retracing along the line alternating from the right side and then the left side so the repeat is not lopsided.

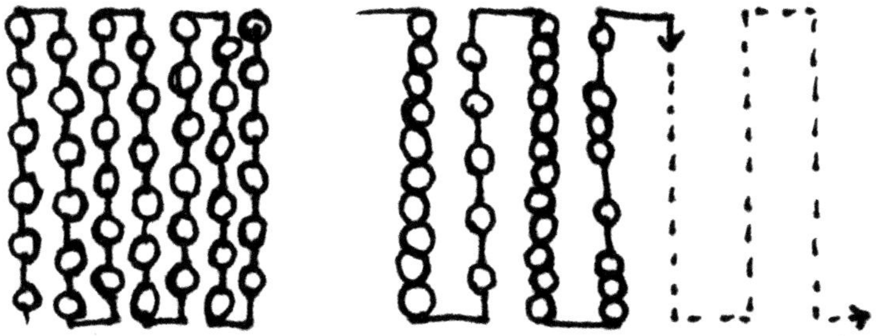

Coaching

Selecting the Best Notebook for Doodling

Dara's doodle books are as varied as her doodles. She likes to keep things simple. When she was an elementary school teacher, she used to teach her students the KISS principle: *Keep It Simple, Sweetie.* Most of her doodle books have come from dollar stores. We encourage you to focus on the purpose of the books—to get your hands and mind fine-tuned to create designs on your quilts. Try a few until you find what works the best for you. For how to select the best notebook for your needs, see Notebooks (page 11).

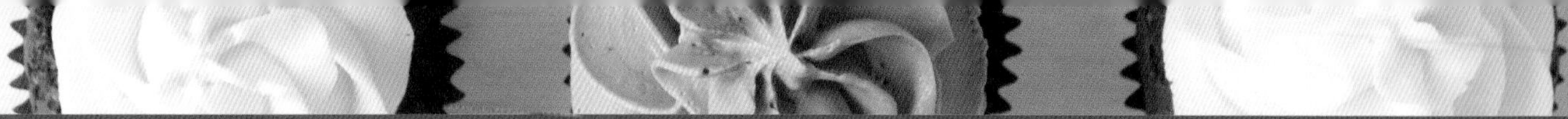

DAY 3: SWIRLS

Prompt

Have you ever thought about all the ways there are to make a swirl?

There are round swirls, linear swirls, all different sizes of swirls. Let's think about shapes we could turn into swirls. Hearts, stars, suns, leaves … anything with a hollow center could contain a swirl, really. What could a swirl become? A snail? A lollipop? A flower? Wind? A tail? A flourish on another shape like a heart or a letter? Absolutely! All these and more are possibilities.

There are swirls in the world all around us. Puddles, ferns, and hair are just a few of the places they turn up. Think about a dancer twirling ribbons and what a beautiful swirl the ribbons can make. When it comes to doodling swirls, we really hope you'll think outside the box … or actually, the swirl.

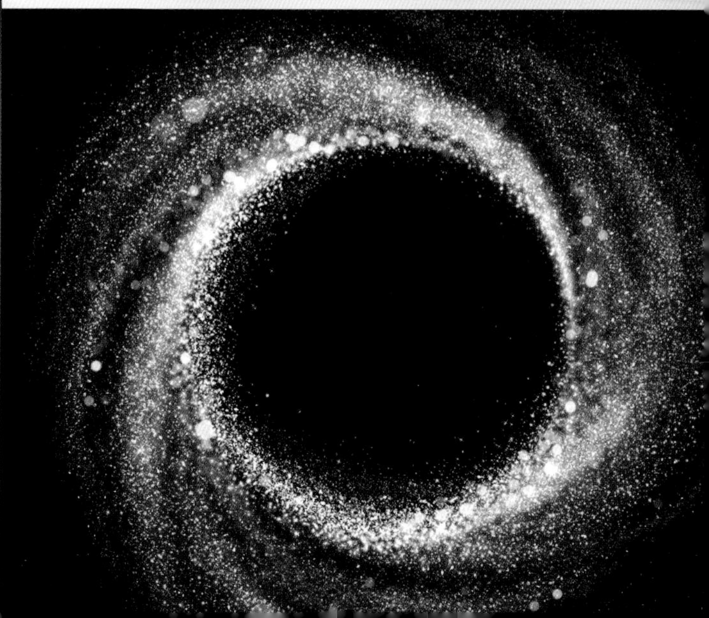

Technical Assistance

Let's refer back to our loose change analogy from Day 2: Circles (page 15). You can also think of swirls as a handful of loose change. They come in various sizes but they're all perfectly round. When you're making swirls, they can also be a variety of sizes. The number of spirals inside your swirls can also vary. In fact, a little variation in the sizes of your swirls can make your overall pattern more interesting. However, the spacing between your lines needs to be consistent and this takes practice.

As you spiral into the center of your swirl, keep it open and loose. Think about the space you're going to want between the lines of your finished swirl and double that. Over time, you'll get a good sense of the amount of space you need. Also, remember to leave space at the bottom of your swirl when you start to spiral in. You're going to need that space when it comes time to exit.

When you get to the center of your spiral, go ahead and pause. You have two options for exiting. You can echo inside the cup of the C-shape or you can echo around the outside of the C-shape. We recommend you echo inside the cup of the C-shape. This creates a much prettier swirl.

Applications

1 RAINBOW SWIRL: Start on a border or outside edge. Draw a swirl following the guidelines in Technical Assistance (page 19). As you exit, echo all the way back around the outside curve of the swirl until you meet back up with the border. Now, reverse directions and use the line you just drew to travel to the next area where you want a swirl. Draw another swirl, echoing around the outside edge of the swirl until the line meets up with the first swirl. Now travel briefly along the outside line of the first swirl and then exit to create an echo around the second swirl. When the echo line meets up with the first swirl on the opposite side, you can either start another swirl, or travel along the outside edge of any echo lines until you get to the area where you want another swirl. Keep this up until you have filled the space with as many swirls as you want.

---

2 ECHO SWIRL: The difference between the echo swirl and the rainbow swirl is that with the echo swirl, you never want your lines to touch. So, this time, as you exit the swirl, go ahead and start into the next swirl any time before the line can intersect with the border. When you finish this swirl, you can echo around it, and the first swirl if you'd like to travel to another area. When you come to a place where 2 swirls meet, you can echo that space with an angle or with a curve.

3 **SWIRL HOOK:** Adding a hook gives a traditional swirl a new personality. Begin by making a traditional swirl. As you exit the swirl, however, don't continue to echo the outside edge. Instead, briefly echo the curve you created when you were first entering the swirl. Before you go too far, reverse directions and echo the curve you just made. You've now created your hook. Now echo the outside of your swirl as you normally would. You can start your next swirl hook right away or echo to a different area and repeat the design.

Coaching

Spacing

Spacing is so important in free-motion quilting. Good quilting is as much about the areas you leave unquilted as it is about the areas you decide to quilt. When your spacing is consistent, those unquilted areas look smooth and even.

It might improve your spacing if you think of free-motion quilting as like driving a car. When you drive, you learn to look in the distance—where you're headed—rather than at the road right in front of your car or to either side. The way your eyes and muscles work together in free-motion quilting is the same. When you're new to free-motion quilting, you probably tend to keep your eyes glued to the area you are quilting. This often makes your lines wobble and you have less control. Start to build the habit of looking ahead at your target and you will find that your peripheral vision and your muscles do a really good job of keeping your quilting evenly spaced between any lines you need to echo or travel past.

DAY 4: LEAVES

Prompt

We love leaves!

They are perfect for doodling and free-motion quilting. We often see them in clusters, so they look natural when we cluster them together for background fillers. Strings of single leaves or leaves on vines look great in borders. And, of course, a couple of leaves perfectly complement any flower.

We connect leaves to countries and cultures: A maple leaf is associated with Canada, a ginkgo reminds us of Japan, and a laurel is often related with Greece. Leaves also remind us of holidays or seasons, such as holly for Christmas or oak leaves for fall. No matter the theme or style of the quilt, we can confidently say, "There's a leaf for that."

Technical Assistance

Go for a walk and gather leaves from a variety of trees and plants. First, look at their stems. Some leaves are simple, with a single leaf growing from one stem, and others are compound, with sets of leaves branching out from both sides of a center stem or with leaves radiating out from the top of a main stem. When you doodle or quilt leaves, you usually start with the stem and the center vein and then build the leaf around that. Draw your stem and center vein with a bit of a curve to make your leaves look natural.

Notice the veins branching out from the center vein. To add more detail to your leaves, draw some branching veins. They're easy to make by drawing short, slightly curved strokes out and then back from both sides of the center vein. You can branch out more and make your veins complex, if you want, but remember that every leaf you make needs to have similar complexity. This requires time and patience.

When you finish your veins, travel back down your center vein to the base of your leaf to create the outside shape. Starting at the base, work your way around the outside edge of the leaf, from left to right. With complex leaves, such as a maple leaf, for example, don't try to recreate every angle and detail of the outside line—there are just too many. Capture the main curves and angles as you follow the outside shape of the leaf with your eyes. If you decided to draw branching veins and you are building your leaf around them, notice that the parts of the leaf that protrude out the farthest from the center vein are echoing and encasing the branching veins that you drew. Let the veins guide you.

Applications

1 **HEARTS-SHAPED LEAVES:** Draw a short, slightly curved stem. Working from left to right, draw the first half of a heart, starting with the rounded part and stopping at the tip. Draw the center vein of your leaf by traveling back to the stem. Draw the other half of the heart, merging with your center vein at the pointy tip of your heart leaf. Continue your line in a curvy meander until you get to an area where you can begin another heart leaf.

---

2 **OAK LEAVES:** Start by making a slightly curved, branching line for the vein of the leaf. As you travel back down the center vein line, create branches in the vein by drawing small curved lines on both sides of the center vein in a smooth motion, out and then back to the center. Next draw curvy lobes along one side of the vein—like round puzzle pieces—with each lobe enveloping a branch of the vein. Loop around the top of the center vein. If you'd like, draw a small scallop, a large scallop, and another small scallop around the top to mimic the natural appearance of an oak leaf. Draw lobes along the other side of the vein, mirroring the first side of the leaf, until you merge your lines at the base. If you'd like, you can echo your leaf for more emphasis. Travel to the next leaf using curvy lines and swirls.

3 **ECHOED LEAF FILL:** Draw a basic leaf shape, rounded at the bottom and pointed at the tip. Reverse directions and echo the leaf, merging your lines when you come back to the starting point. From the base of the first leaf, curve out into a second leaf shape. The place where the inner shape of the second leaf ends will come to a point that merges either with the first leaf or with the border. Reverse directions, echo back and repeat the steps from the first leaf. Continue this simple design throughout the area you need to fill. You can echo more than once to travel or for effect.

Coaching

Free-Motion Aspirations

Whether you aspire to become a proficient quilter or to become an expert quilter, you will create beautiful quilts. This challenge fulfills all aspirations!

If your purpose in completing the challenge is to finish up a stack of simple quilts for family and friends, then aspiring to become a proficient free-motion quilter is probably right for you. You can stick to simple, traditional free-motion designs. This doesn't take away your creative license, however. You'll find that you can be quite creative as a proficient free-motion quilter.

If you plan to quilt for competitions or you plan to do custom work for clients who compete, you should aim to become an expert free-motion quilter. You'll need to learn more complex designs and hone your precision.

DAY 5: HOLLY

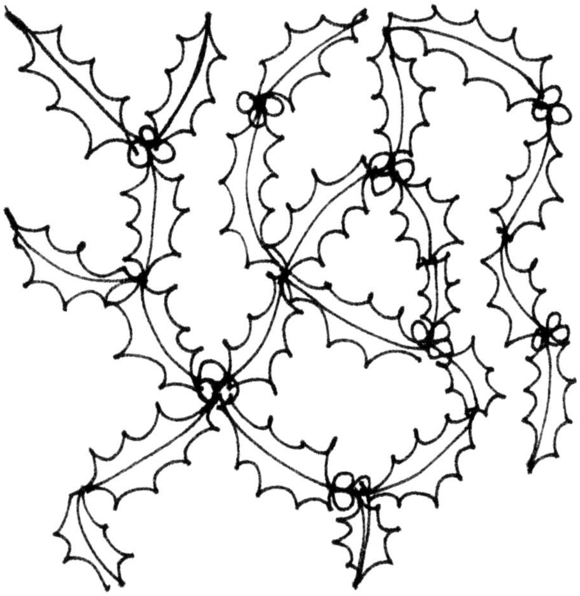

Prompt

It's time to focus on one of our favorite seasonal leaves: holly.

Holly brings back special memories for Dara. It's a design she mastered and quilted early in her free-motion quilting journey. Dara's cousin showed her two incredible Christmas quilt tops one day and Dara was super-impressed with them. She had just started to feel confident enough in her free-motion quilting to ask her cousin if she could have the privilege of quilting them for her. She was thrilled when her cousin agreed and after hours of practicing, she was delighted that she could create some beautiful motifs for her cousin's quilts.

So many of the quilts we create are seasonal. Practice a few holly motifs so you are ready for all the holiday quilts that are sure to come your way. There's a good chance you're going to have warm memories of quilting holly motifs in treasured family quilts, just like Dara.

Technical Assistance

Holly looks complicated but, with a few rules, you will be off and doodling in no time. There are several ways to create the leaf design. Let's practice the most common first. Once you've got the basic leaf down, think about ways you can incorporate pine boughs, candy canes, fluffy bows, or anything else that reminds you of the holidays. Are you starting to see how much fun holly can be?

Start with a simple, slightly curved vein out and then back. Now, draw a series of 3 or more inverted scallops that echo around the vein, ending the first side of the holly leaf with a point that lands above the upper tip of the vein.

Draw inverted scallops down the other side of the vein, mirroring the scallops on the first side. Merge the end of the final scallop with the vein at the base where you began.

Applications

1 **CLUSTERS OF HOLLY WITH BERRIES:** Start with a berry, in the center of the cluster. For each berry, draw a small circle first, then draw a swirl inside the circle by spiraling in and then out on the same line. Draw at least 3 berries before you move on to the leaves. From the last berry, draw a vein radiating out and then finish the first leaf as described above. Echo around the berries to another area before you start your second leaf. Repeat this process until you have at least 3 holly leaves around the berries.

2 **HOLLY GARLAND BORDER DESIGN:** For this design, you're going to draw the holly leaf in a different order from the way we drew it in Technical Assistance (page 27). Draw a short vein that travels roughly lengthwise inside the border. Next, draw inverted scallops, traveling back along one side of the vein, merging the final scallop with the vein at the base. Do the same along the other side of the vein, merging the last scallop with the vein tip. Echo the scallops, again merging the last echo with the tip of the first. Your first leaf is complete. Now continue to draw a wavy line along the center of the border to create the string of the garland. Continue the line until you are ready for another leaf. Once you've got the basic garland design down, try adding loops, swirls, and berries to the string of the garland and next to the holly leaves.

---

3 **HOLLY LEAF MEANDER:** Draw a basic holly leaf. Echo once around the leaf. You can begin the next leaf from the tip of the first or you can use the outside echo of the first leaf to travel to another area and begin a second leaf. Echo all the leaves once. Try drawing some of your leaves peeking out from under other leaves. Continue until the entire area is filled.

Coaching

Manageable Milestones

Now that you know "why" you want to take this doodle challenge, it's time to create a plan. Start by setting a few manageable milestones to help measure your progress. You don't need to know every step you're going to take in advance. You can focus on one milestone at a time and simply plan the steps you'll need to take for that part of your journey. As you reach each milestone, give yourself an opportunity to reflect, celebrate your accomplishments, and create a plan for reaching your next milestone. Can you see how focusing on one milestone at a time can help you avoid being overwhelmed?

DAY 6: BUBBLES

Prompt

Okay, wait. Aren't circles and bubbles the same?

Yes and no. Let's think about the characteristics that make a bubble different from a circle. A bubble can float, a bubble can pop, a bubble can hold a reflection. Bubbles are light, airy, fun, iridescent, and sometimes fizzy. We associate bubbles with small children, with playfulness, and with bath time.

As you're thinking about ways to render bubbles in continuous-line doodles, think about the characteristics that make a bubble uniquely a bubble. Try to incorporate some of those things into your doodles and you will find that your bubble doodles take on a character that is unmistakably bubbly.

Technical Assistance

One way to differentiate a bubble from a circle is to add a reflection or a highlight to it. Once you've drawn a circle, draw a line curving into the inside, closely following the outline of the circle. Turn this line into a kind of arched rectangle and there you have it—a reflection. If you include reflections in your bubbles, be sure to put one in roughly the same area in each bubble you draw.

We also like to think of bubbles as being more sociable than circles. They often come in bunches and they don't mind getting right up into each other's space. You'll often see bubbles overlapping or bubbles within bubbles.

Also, you may have noticed that bubbles aren't necessarily perfectly round. When you see bubbles in clusters or connected to something else, the side that connects is always flat. Try connecting your bubbles with an overlap or a flat connection to make them more realistic.

Applications

1 **BUBBLE CLUSTERS:** These are similar to circle clusters, except your bubbles can overlap or be drawn inside one another. Draw a circle. When you draw a second circle, try to make it overlap the first. When you draw a third circle, put it inside the second one. Keep going to create a cluster of bubbles. Try to keep the edge flat where 2 bubbles join.

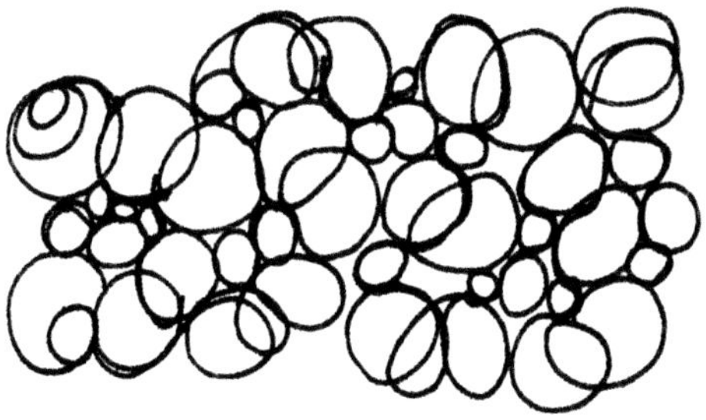

2 **FLOATING BUBBLE BORDER:** Draw a bubble with a reflection. Travel back to the outside line of the bubble on the same line you used when you came into the reflection. Next draw a loopy line, traveling along the inside of the border until you come to the place where you want to draw the next bubble. Repeat this along the length of the border.

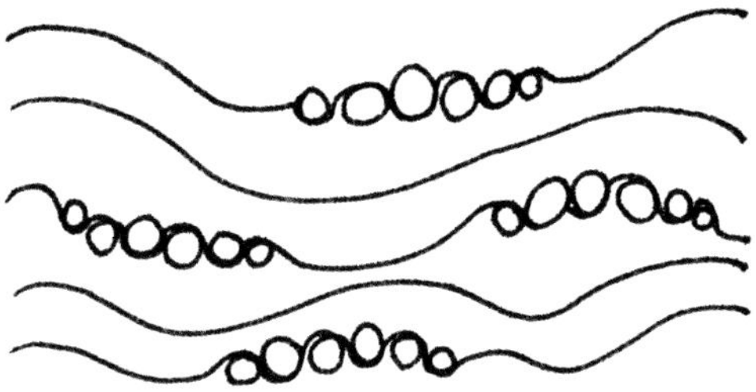

3 **BUBBLES IN A STREAM:** This design mimics bubbles in a stream of water. Draw a wavy line, broken up occasionally by strings of circles. To make your circles look like bubbles instead of a string of pearls, vary the sizes of the bubbles and flatten the connecting edges just a bit or overlap the edges. Draw another wavy line under the first, it doesn't need to echo the first line, but it can, if you'd like. Wherever you drew bubbles in the first line, curve the second line around the bubbles like water flowing around a small island. Continue drawing wavy lines, throwing in random strings of bubbles. Draw some lines without bubbles to space the bubbles out a bit.

Coaching

Spacing

As you create your doodles, think about the space between your lines. When it comes time to stitch your designs on a quilt, will you want to quilt it the same as you drew it? You might decide to spread out your design and create more space between the lines when you quilt it. Open and loose quilting creates a nice, supple drape in your quilt.

When you plan your spacing, be aware that each type of batting has its own recommendations for space between quilting. Check the packaging or check your batting manufacturer's website for the recommended spacing. As a general rule, plan your designs so that you don't leave any unquilted spaces larger than 3″ in circumference or smaller than about ¼″.

DAY 7: TWIST

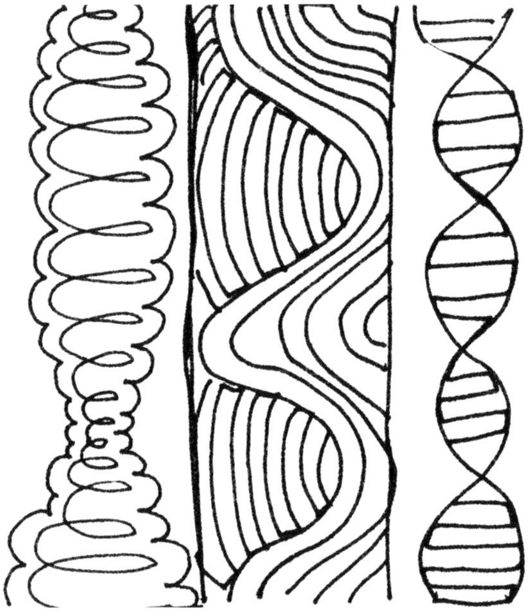

Prompt

So many quilts and quilting designs are inspired by a twist.

When it comes to famous twists in quilting, a twisted bargello quilt is almost always the showstopper. Do an internet search of the words "bargello quilt" to see examples of this beautiful style of quilt. When we look at these quilts, we know the pattern isn't really twisting, but we're always willing to suspend our belief as our eyes follow the twists and turns the pattern creates. The optical illusion makes us feel like we're spinning down a playground slide.

We can create the same types of optical illusions with our quilting designs. Do a little research online and you'll see lots of ways to create the feeling of motion and lead your viewers eyes through your quilts with a playful twist.

Technical Assistance

You can create the illusion of a twist with a series of S-curves. You'll probably find it easier to learn S-curves if you draw some guidelines first. Draw 2 solid parallel lines across the width of your paper from left to right, about 3″ apart. Imagine that these 2 lines represent the upper and lower edges of a quilt border. Divide the space between these borders with 3 horizontal dashed lines, as shown in the illustration below.

Start at the left side of your page. From the lower solid line, draw a line, from left to right, that travels gradually upward. When you near the first dashed line, start to curve the line more sharply up until it reaches about a 45° angle. Continue at this angle through the middle dashed line. As you near the upper dashed line, curve the line more sharply to the right and smoothly merge it with the upper solid line.

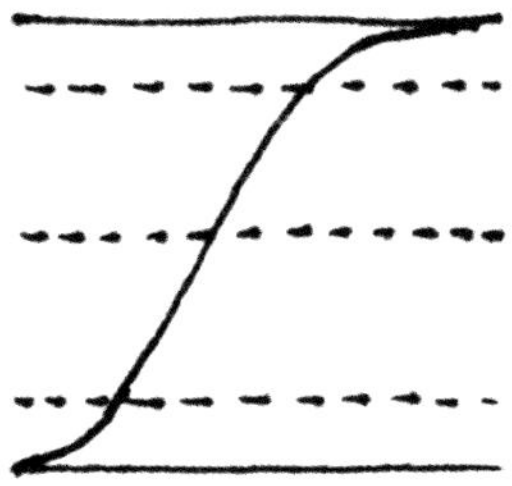

You've completed your first S-curve.

For the second S-curve, repeat the steps for first in reverse order, from right to left, so that you echo the first S-curve. Alternate, drawing S-curves traveling up and from left to right, and then traveling down and right to left, as you fill the border. After you've drawn several S-curves, your border will start to look like a twisted rope.

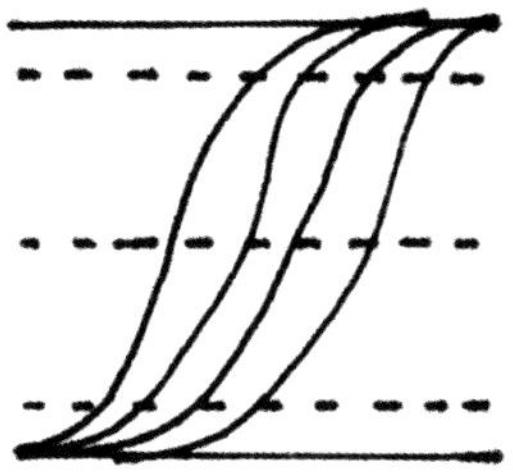

Here's one final tip for filling a border with twisted lines: Maintain the 45° angle in your lines as you cross the middle of the border so your S-curves flow and twist elegantly.

Applications

1 SIMPLE CABLE BORDER DESIGN: Mark your paper with 2 solid lines, 3″ apart, as you did for practicing S-curves. Divide the area between the solid lines into roughly equal lengthwise sections using dashed lines. The widths of these sections will determine how loose or tight your twists will appear to be. For this exercise, make each lengthwise section about as wide as it is tall. Then, mark between 4 and 6 sections.

Starting on the left, draw a line in the first lengthwise section, going from the bottom dashed line to the top dashed line. The line should curve slightly in the middle. Then, draw a downward curve through the second section that ends at the lower dashed line. Continue drawing the up and down curved lines to the end of the guideline border.

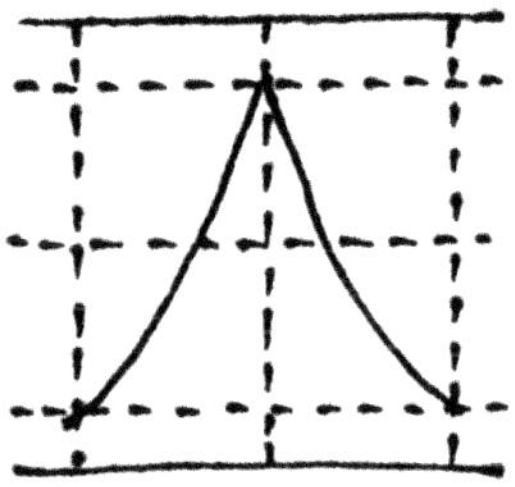

Travel up the right margin of the guidelines to the top or bottom dashed line (depending on where the curve ended from the previous step). Draw a curved line, as in the previous step, back through each section. These lines should cross the first lines at the center dashed lines (as shown). Continue until reaching the left guideline border.

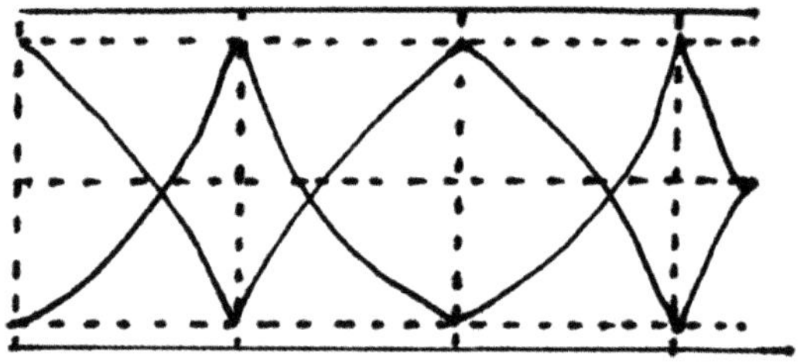

2 TWISTED SQUARE: Grab a ruler and draw a 6″ × 6″ square that runs parallel to the bottom of your paper. After you've connected the fourth corner of the square, travel along the first line you drew in the square for about 1″. From here, draw a straight line to a point about 1″ past the next corner of this first square. Draw a second line from this point to a point about 1″ past the next corner, and so on, until you have closed up the second square within the first square.

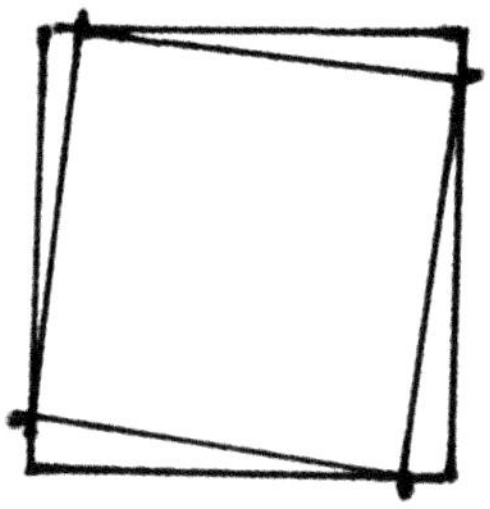

Travel along the first line of the second square and stop after 1″. Follow the steps in the previous paragraph when you drew the second square to complete a third square within the second square. Continue these steps, drawing squares within squares until the center square is about 1″ on all sides.

Coaching

Dry Erase Board

One of the most common challenges that comes up in continuous-line doodling is hand cramps and fatigue. When we're doodling in this way, we sometimes forget to pause to rest our hand. Some of us tense up and press down harder than we need to with our pen. We don't notice what we're doing until our hand cramps up and we feel the pain.

If any of this sounds like you, we'd like to suggest a small change that will probably make a big difference. Try doodling on a dry erase board. You've probably written on a dry erase board before, so you know how smoothly and effortlessly dry erase markers glide across the surface. With this approach, you can practice more with less stress to your hand.

If you come up with a design you love, take a picture of it or try duplicating it in your notebook so that you don't lose it when you erase your board. Give a dry erase board a try and see what you think. It's an easy fix that could be a key to your success.

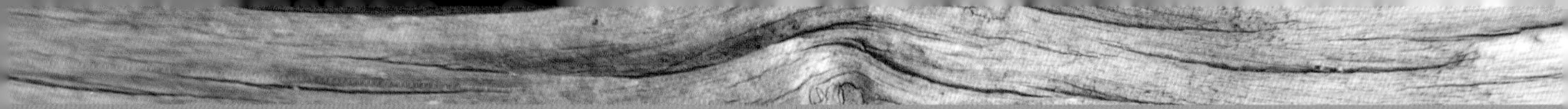

DAY 8: ECHOES

Prompt

What would free-motion quilting be like without echoes?

We honestly can't imagine it. Echoing is such a staple of free-motion quilting. We use echoes in almost every quilt we make as they often become parts of a larger pattern. We use them to travel from one area to another, to emphasize designs in the quilt top, to emphasize our own quilting designs, and even just to fill up space. With a little practice, echoes nearly always make your quilting look fantastic.

Technical Assistance

Your echoes will look best if you can keep the space between them consistent. There are exceptions to this rule but, for now, focus on consistent spacing.

Of course, if you are curious about inconsistent spacing, try the application 2. Triple Echo Patterned Flower (page 38). Other examples of inconsistent spacing are when your echoes need to merge at each end (check out Karen McTavish's famous technique, "McTavishing," on the internet), or when you are drawing swirls and waves for wind or organic elements like grass. These echoes sometimes look best if they merge at places and are consistently inconsistent.

But let's get back to consistent spacing in our echoes. We'll do a simple exercise to practice. Begin by drawing 3 connecting circles.

Travel out from between 2 circles. This will be the only echo line that connects. As you echo the first circle, let the line gradually increase in distance away from the circle until it is about ½″ away. From this point until you are finished, try to keep the spacing between echoes about ½″.

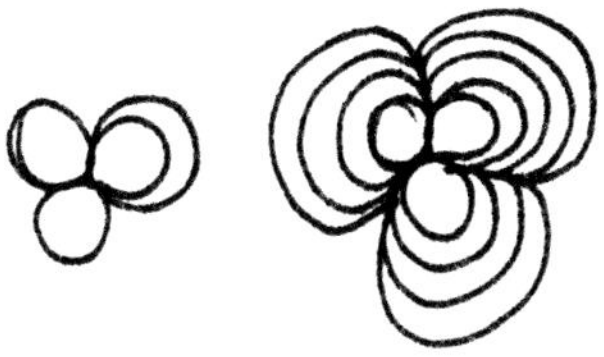

Once you are satisfied with your ½″ echoes and to help improve your hand-eye coordination, try doing this exercise again but spacing your lines about ¼″ apart. Repeat this exercise a third time with 1″ spacing.

Applications

1 **ECHOES THAT MEET AN EDGE:** If you echo anything long enough, your echoes are going to run into a border, another design, or go off the edge of your quilt. What should you do when that happens? Let's practice.

Draw a 4″ square on the paper. Then, draw 3 connected circles near a corner inside the square. Begin echoing the circles until your echo line meets an edge of the square.

Then, travel along the edge of the square a short distance and echo the circles again in the reverse direction to fill the square.

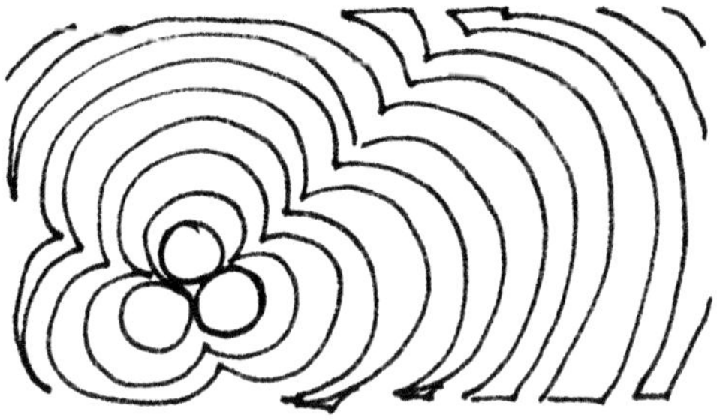

2 **TRIPLE ECHO PATTERNED FLOWER:** For this design, we're going to break the "equal spacing rule." Draw a flower with 6 equal-size petals and echo about ¼″ away from and around each petal, merging the echo lines between each petal.

For the second set of echoes, increase the distance between the echo lines to about ½″. Next, do one more set of echoes at ¼″ and another at ½″. Repeat this pattern of echoes several times so that you can clearly see the pattern taking shape around your flower.

Coaching

Tracking Progress

Look objectively at the doodles you made for this exercise. What can you see that you could improve? What are you already doing well? You can also ask yourself questions about how you felt today as you doodled. What was easy? What was hard? Write down specific questions to ask yourself in the future, such as, *On the whole, are my transition lines becoming smoother and less wobbly than they were two months ago?*

Make notes in the margins by your doodles. Date your doodles and hang on to them. Look back at your past work regularly. You will probably always see things you want to improve. We all do. Just don't let any progress go unnoted. Celebrate every victory and use this as a time to show yourself some love!

DAY 9: STARS

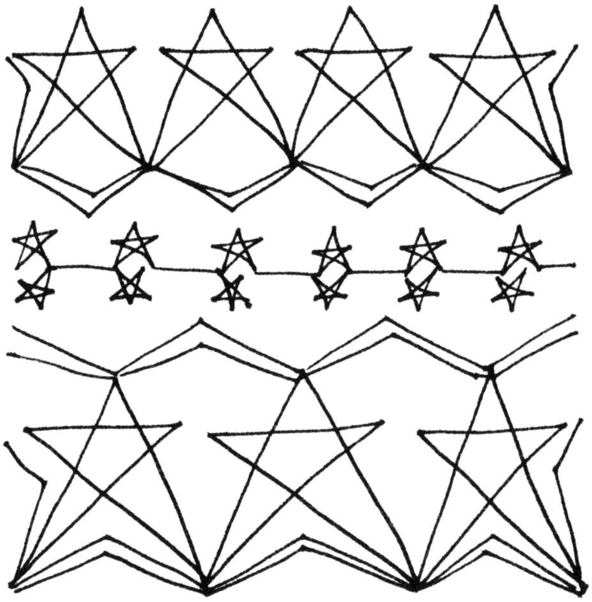

Prompt

When you see a star what does it mean to you?

If you're a U.S. citizen, you might think of the Fourth of July and patriotism. Around the world, Christians associate stars with Christmas. If you're Jewish, the Star of David probably reminds you of your heritage and the State of Israel. If you're Islamic, you probably use a Star and Crescent on your flag. It seems that every nation and culture places symbolic meaning in stars.

We use stars in medical symbols, ratings, achievement awards, military honors, and so much more. They pop up on barns, in punctuation, and on walks of fame. Stars might be the most universal symbol on this planet—and beyond.

Technical Assistance

Five-pointed stars are great for free-motion quilting because you have probably already been drawing them for years with a continuous line. You can turn them any direction you want and you always know you're going to end up at the same point where you started, which saves you from having to figure out where you're going to exit the design. We're going to show you two ways to form and use five-pointed stars in Applications (below).

Another type of star that's easy to use in free-motion quilting is an asterisk. If you're using it in a meander or along a straight line, your line can become a part of the asterisk. Just stop where you want the asterisk to be, then draw an X. Think about the legs of the X as branching out from your original line, with each leg being about equal in length. Then, draw a perpendicular line crossing through the middle of the X. Exit the asterisk across from the original travel line.

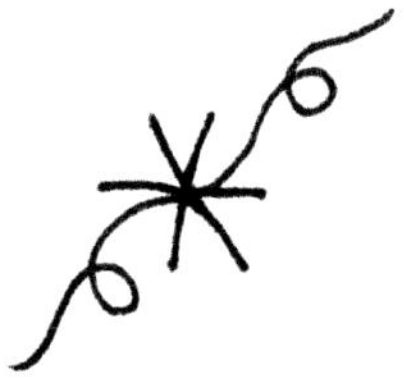

Applications

1 CRISSCROSS STAR MEANDER: Start by drawing a loopy, meandering line. When you're ready, make the peak of the first star at about a 45° angle so it looks like an upside-down capital V. We've labeled the illustration (A, B, C) to help with the following steps.

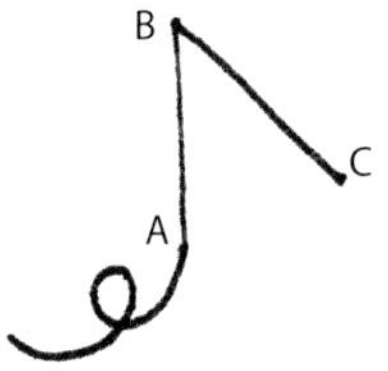

Starting from C, draw a line that intersects A and B and stops at D. Then draw a line that crosses below point B and ends at E. Finally, draw a line from point E back to point A.

Your first star is complete. Travel to another area using a loopy meander and then doodle another star. Try to orient your stars in multiple directions, including upside down.

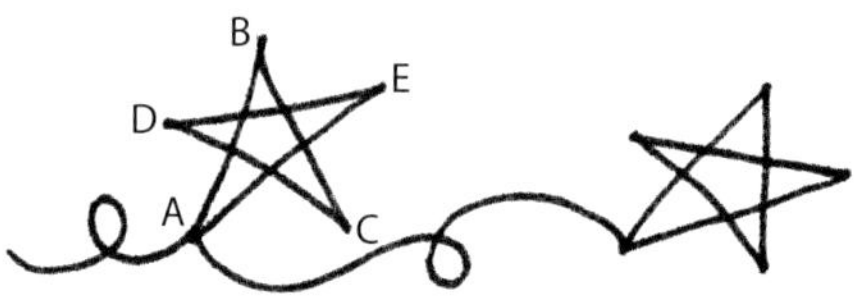

2 TWO-PASS STAR BORDER: Here's another way to form the five-pointed star. Before you begin, draw 2 solid lines, using a ruler, across the width of the paper to represent a border. You should have 1″ or more space between the lines.

For the first part of the design, draw a zigzagging chevron, beginning at the bottom border on the left side of the page and going up and then down, up and then down at about a 30° angle each time. Try to keep the angle consistent. Stop at the bottom border when you get near the right side of the paper.

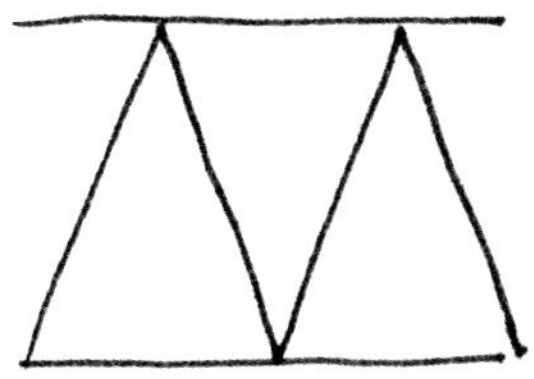

The peaks of the chevrons are going to become the peaks of the stars. Label the points of the chevron A, B, and C, as with 1. Crisscross Star Meander (previous page). Then add D and E (as shown).

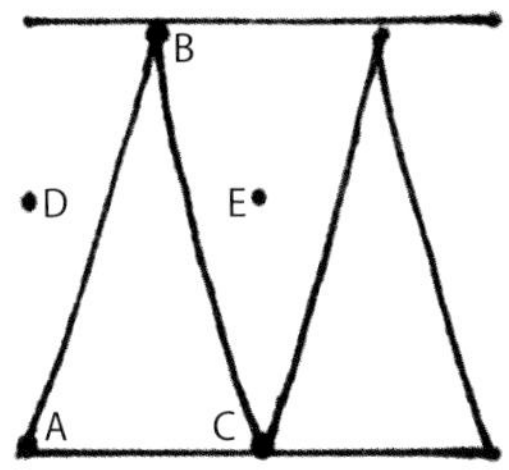

Draw a line from point A to E, then from point E to D, then ending at point C.

Working from left to right, continue across the border in this manner. You can decide if you want your stars to share their points D and E. If they meet at these points, the stars look like they're holding hands across the border.

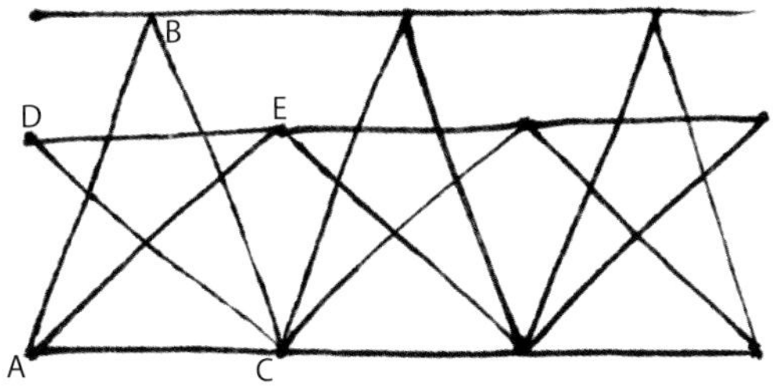

Coaching

Planning Ahead

When you put even a little time into planning out how you are going to achieve your goals, you see more progress. Even if you don't end up completing your goal, you'll notice you go farther and accomplish more than you accomplish when you don't plan at all.

So, schedule time to do the work. Then, set deadlines to finish certain tasks. If you find yourself nearing your deadline and you haven't progressed as much as you'd like, you can decide whether to push yourself harder or to extend your deadline. Just don't keep pushing your date back indefinitely. Setting and honoring deadlines creates a "light at the end of the tunnel" effect. When we know our task has an end date, we can persevere through the hard parts and see it through.

DAY 10: TRIANGLES

Prompt

Ah, the triangle.

This shape takes Amy (way) back to high school geometry. In geometry, triangles are magical. Any polygon (a shape made with straight lines and three or more angles) can be divided into triangles. Their angles give us the information we need to determine size and distance. But now we're getting into territory where Amy's memory gets foggier. . . .

Let's talk about symbolism again—an area where Amy feels more confident. A triangle can represent a trinity, which is something that comes in threes, such as the Bee Gees. It also represents an ascending pathway, such as Egyptian pyramids that seem like a path up to heaven.

Coming back down to earth, where do we see triangles in everyday life? How about the play symbol on our computers? There are also triangle-shape mountains, road signs, arrows, and pennants. And finally, Amy's favorite trinity (and her favorite way to consume geometry): ice cream cones, cheese wedges, and slices of pizza.

Technical Assistance

Triangles are a free-motion quilter's best friend. Think about it. . . . We can decompose any polygon we encounter into triangles—and we encounter all kinds of polygons in quilts—think hexagons, octagons, quadrilaterals, nonagons . . . you get the idea. Dividing your space with triangles is very easy to do. To practice this in your doodles, draw any polygon (an enclosed shape with angles connected by straight lines) and draw lines connecting the point of one angle to another. You can also mark points between the angles of the polygons and further divide the shape by connecting these points. When you're done, you can leave the triangles as they are or fill them up with additional designs.

When you encounter polygons in your quilts, think about how you could quilt out the space inside them with triangle shapes. Dividing up the space in your quilts in this way often creates secondary patterns that you might not have known were possible. These secondary patterns, in turn, often create pleasing new paths for our eyes to follow.

A fun exercise is to draw out a traditional quilt pattern. Start with something simple, such as nine-patches, which usually alternate a background and a foreground color of 9 equal-size squares. Draft out the quilt in 2 colors, then come in with a pencil or marker in another color and divide the spaces in the pattern into triangles. When you're finished, take a step back and look for the secondary patterns you've created. You'll probably find more than one. You can even go in again with another colored pen or marker and divide the space into triangles in a different way.

Applications

1 **TRIANGLE ECHOES AND FILL:** To get started, draw 2 triangles, base to base. You can use a ruler or estimate. Draw a 4″ dashed line across the paper. Bisect the line with a dashed line that's about 2″ long and creates a cross with the first line. Connect all the outside points with solid lines. Notice that when you join 2 triangles, base to base, they form a larger diamond shape. Next, we're going to echo the larger diamond shape.

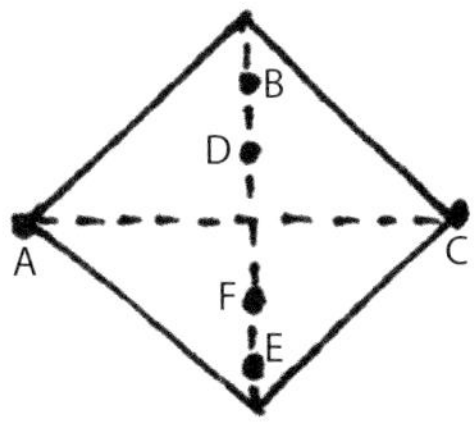

Mark a point ¼″ inside an obtuse angle of the diamond shape. Mark another point ¼″ inside from the first point. Do the same inside the opposite obtuse angle. Label the points (as shown).

Next, draw a line from A to B to C and then travel backward from C to D to A. You've created the first 2 echoes. Let's echo the other side of the diamond by drawing from A to E to C and then backward from C to F and back to A again.

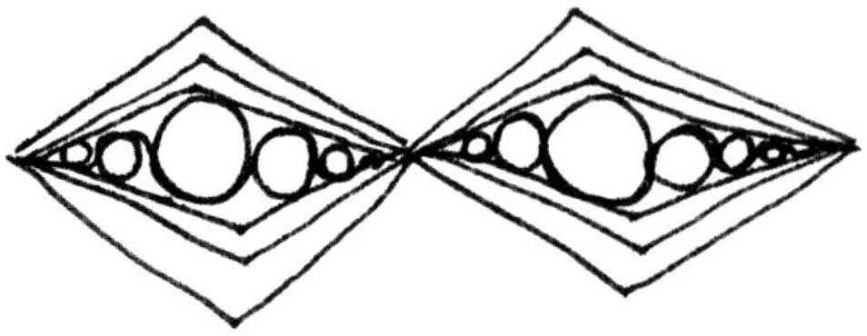

That's it! You can now fill the center of the diamond with any design you like (such as a string of pearls) in order to travel back to point C and exit. Try drawing several connecting diamonds with a string of pearls in the middle.

---

2 **TRIANGLE TANGLE:** If you're looking for a geometric background filler, look no further. This one will fill your space with glorious angles.

Draw a 6″ square on the paper. Draw a straight line from the left border of the square, traveling toward the center. After you've gone 1″–2″, draw a triangle that starts with an acute angle, traveling right to left, and then another acute angle that travels up and crosses the first line you drew.

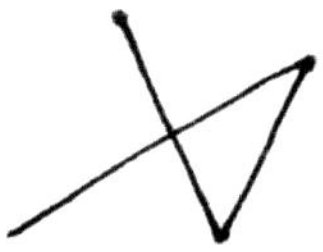

Continue past the first triangle with a straight line until you are ready to draw another triangle or until you are ready to draw another angle that will help you travel to a different area. It's really fun to fill up an area this way.

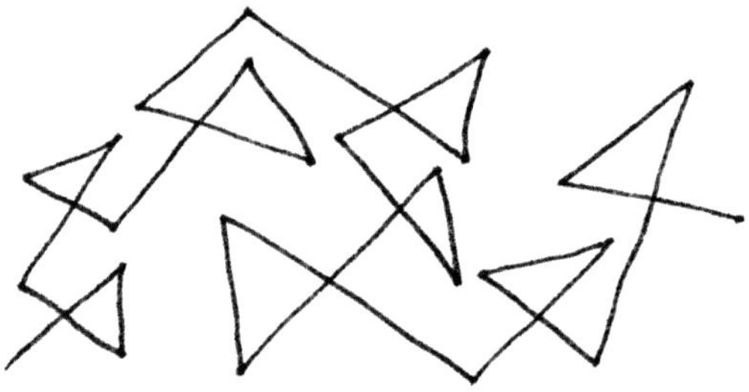

Coaching

Scale

Scale can be relative. Use that to your advantage. If you want to make something look large in your free-motion quilting, all you need to do is put smaller things near it. If you put a flower into a meander and you want it to seem large, put small flowers in the meander around it or even just make the meander small and tight. Your flower will seem large by comparison.

DAY 11: CLOUDS

Prompt

Think about things that go along with clouds, such as wind, birds, the sun, the moon, airplanes, treetops, or mountaintops. You can take anything that reaches up into the sky and work it in with a cloud design.

You can also experiment with doodling different types of clouds. The clouds we usually draw are cumulus clouds. Find pictures online of cirrus clouds, stratus clouds, or any other type of clouds and see if you can recreate their shapes and attributes in your doodles.

Technical Assistance

Let's go over a basic cloud shape. Imagine you are drawing a bunch of scallop shapes that work their way around a circular center and then reconnect where they started. You can draw as many scallops as you want, but more than 4 will make your cloud seem puffier. Your scallops don't have to be the same size. Try varying the sizes and see what you think.

Now let's practice something more complicated. We'll call them "compound clouds." Draw a cloud the same way you just did, but this time stop when you are about three-quarters complete. Now travel back along your scallops a little—go about 2½ scallops back. From here, branch out and draw another cloud that envelops the right side of the first, incomplete cloud. Finish this second cloud by merging it up with the bottom of the first cloud. You can create a large cluster of clouds using this method.

To create a cloudy sky design, fill a space with random clouds that are joined by curvy lines or loopy meanders. Try echoing the clouds for another effect.

Applications

1 **SWIRLY CLOUDS:** Create a swirl that spirals into the center and then travels back out along the same line. Then, draw a couple of scallops traveling away from the spiral and create a smaller spiral at the end of the second scallop.

Continue drawing scallops and spirals, working your way around the first spiral to create a cloud shape. When you're happy with how it looks, merge your line into any other place in the cloud.

2 **WIND AND CLOUDS FILL:** Let's practice mixing wind and clouds together. Start with a wavy line that ends in a spiral to create the wind. Fill out the wind shape by echoing above and below the wavy line and the spiral.

Draw 2 or 3 more wavy spirals connected to the first. Then, draw a cloud away from the wind with a series of scallops. You can end the cloud by joining it to the wind after you've circled around a bit with the scallops.

Add as much wind and as many clouds as you like, filling in the area as you see fit. If you get into a tight space, throw in some echoes to travel to another area and continue your design.

3 BIRDS AND CLOUDS FILL: This time, you're going to form your clouds a little differently and throw in some birds. Start near the top of the paper, on the left side. Draw a few scallops, moving from left to right. Then draw scallops climbing up and then back down to form a large pouf.

Before your pouf gets down to the level of the first scallops, throw in a bird by drawing 2 scallops straight out to the right and then echoing them, merging the echo with the first of the 2 scallops at the tip.

Then complete the cloud pouf and work your way farther right using more scallops at the same level on the paper as the first scallops. Throw in more poufs with birds coming off them at random places, as you see fit.

When you reach the right edge of the paper, use the margin to travel down and draw another row of clouds and birds moving from the right side of the paper to the left.

Continue adding rows to your cloud and bird fill until you've filled up your space.

Coaching

Large Paper

We predict that, someday, you're going to find yourself standing in front of a large, empty space on a quilt and wondering how in the world to fill it up. Why not problem-solve for that now?

Our favorite way to tackle a large space is to divide and conquer. Start with a large piece of paper, 11″ × 13″ or even larger. Think of interesting, pleasing ways to subdivide the space. Quilting smaller areas can be much less daunting. Or increase the scale of your quilting. Quilts with large backgrounds often also have large pieced designs. You can always quilt large to fill up large areas. It's a good idea to practice doodling on large paper first.

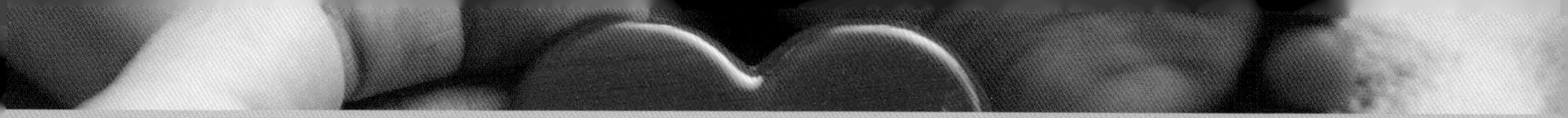

DAY 12: HEARTS

Prompt

Is it possible to think about hearts without thinking about love? Maybe ... but why would we want to? Love, sweetness, kindness, caring—it feels like all our purest and deepest emotions come from our hearts. There's something special about that organ pumping inside our chests.

Of course, Valentine's Day is a time when love is on everyone's minds. Hearts start popping up everywhere and you'll probably find yourself quilting more heart motifs during that time than any other. However, since we so often make quilts as expressions of our love, heart designs can grace our quilting any time of year.

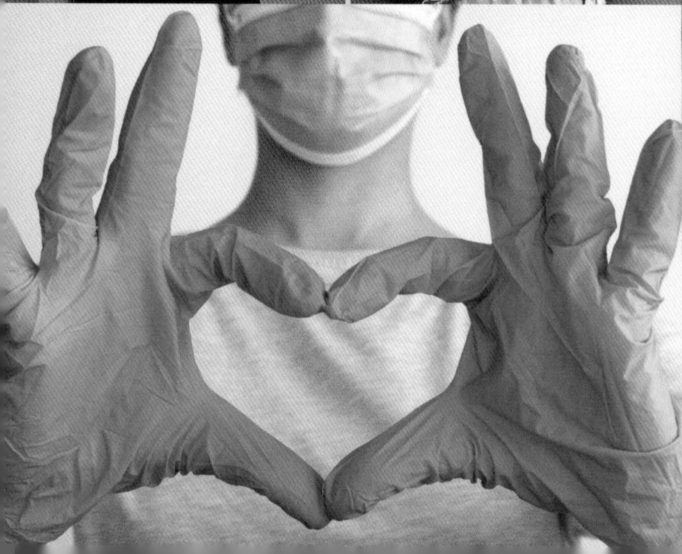

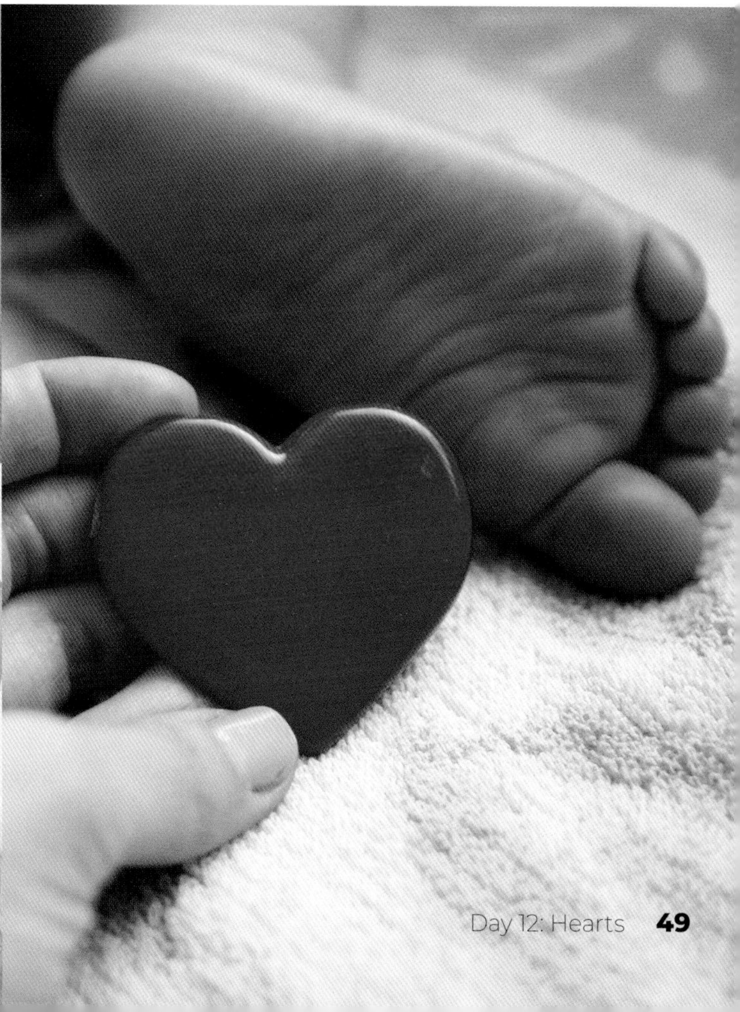

Technical Assistance

Usually, the best place to start drawing a heart is at the point at the bottom or at the point of the V in the upper center. A standard heart shape, with the 2 sides balanced, can be difficult to draw. Let's work on a balanced heart first and then, we'll explore a variation with our application 2. Wonky Hearts Fill (next page).

Starting at the bottom of your heart, draw the left half first. Draw a diagonal line traveling left and upward. When you're ready, imagine your line is curving up and around, forming a half-circle and stopping on the right side of the circle, directly above the point where your heart began.

To form the right half of your heart, reverse what you just did. Imagine a circle on the right side of your heart that is the same size as the rounded part of the left side you just drew. If it helps, you can even draw in a light dashed circle for a guideline. Draw a line up and around the circle. Break away from the circle on the right side and bring your line down at an angle to meet up with the bottom point of the heart.

Applications

1 HEARTS ON A STRING: Draw a vertical line, starting at the lower left edge of the paper, about 1″ to the right of the corner. After you've come up 2″–3″, draw a small heart that is centered above the vertical line you just drew. Close the heart shape at the bottom, then continue traveling up and around the left side of your heart, stopping when you have traced the entire left half.

Then, travel straight up again, continuing in a vertical line until you are ready to draw another heart. With your second heart, draw the right side first and trace around the right side before continuing your vertical line. If you alternate the direction you travel for each heart, the traced line of the heart will alternate. The half of the heart you trace will look heavier than the untraced half, so alternating the direction you travel and the side you trace when you draw your hearts will balance your design.

To finish, draw another line of hearts on a string, starting at the top of the paper and working down to the bottom. Notice that when you draw from top to bottom, you need to start drawing your hearts at the point of the V and end at the base of the heart if you want to keep them all facing up. Stagger out the placement of the hearts so they aren't directly across from the hearts you drew in the first string.

Continue drawing strings of hearts, working across, from left to right on your page until the page is full.

2 **WONKY HEARTS FILL:** Now let's create a more whimsical-looking, lopsided heart design. Start at the bottom of the page and draw the first side of a heart by making a large, curvy hook shape. For the second side, make the curve smaller. When you bring the line down to meet with the point of the heart, curve it inward so that it echoes and kind of nestles into the curve of the left side.

Echo the heart, merging your echo line at the bottom point of the heart. Draw more echoed hearts around the first. Your hearts should curve around each other. Keep them lopsided. You can echo around them more than once, if you like. Use echo lines to travel to unfilled areas when you need to.

Coaching

Scale

Use scale as a tool when you want to create a sense of depth in your quilting. When placing birds in a cloudy sky, for example, vary their sizes and positions. Some of the birds will appear far away and some will seem closer. Your sky will become more interesting and look more natural.

In addition, change up the scale of your quilting to add variety and texture. For many quilts, we want our texture to be even and smooth but that isn't always the case. In a landscape art quilt, for example, you might want to make the ground look rocky and uneven. To do that, use a pebble fill and vary the sizes of your pebbles. The more your pebbles differ in size from large to small, the more uneven and realistic your texture becomes.

DAY 13: SCALE

Prompt

Are you ready for a deep dive into scale? We've coached you on ways to use scale to indicate size and distance. Today, use scale to explore these concepts in more depth.

In addition, why not doodle some literal scales? Try doodling some scaly animals, such as fish, snakes, lizards, or crocodiles. Next, try some musical scales. Challenge yourself to find a logical path for creating musical scales with a continuous line.

Can you think of any scales we haven't already mentioned? If so, what are they and what potential do you think they have for continuous-line doodles? We'd love to see you get creative with scale.

Technical Assistance

With practice, you can change the scale of any free-motion design. This adaptability will make you a more flexible free-motion quilter. You'll be able to vary the size and spacing of your designs to suit the space you're filling.

Go back and review the Day 3 application 2. Echo Swirl (page 20). First, doodle the design on a large scale. Remember to keep the spacing in your swirls consistent, no matter what scale you are doodling in. You'll probably want to keep the spacing between your lines at about ½″. That's a large scale for most quilting. You can quickly and easily fill a whole page with swirl patterns at this size.

Try reducing the scale of your swirls by about half. Keep about ¼″ between the lines of your swirls. What do you think? Are you finding it easy or difficult to change the scale of your design?

Finally, doodle the design at the smallest scale you feel comfortable with. You may notice yourself tensing up at this point. If so, take a deep breath and consciously relax your hand and shoulders. It's a natural reaction to tense up when you're doodling or quilting something on a very small scale. You'll find, however, that you can do beautiful work at a small scale without tensing your body.

Compare the designs you drew at these 3 scales. What do you see that you can improve? Repeat this exercise with various designs. It's a skill builder that will put you on the fast-track to becoming an adroit free-motion quilter at any scale.

Applications

1 MUSICAL NOTE MEANDER: Start with the base of a note. Draw a circle. Once you've closed the circle, travel around it to the right side, if necessary. Draw a straight line up from the right side of the circle, about 3 times longer than its height. Then, draw a hook shape, coming out from and then back to the right side of the top of the line.

Travel a little down the line and draw another hook shape, out and then back. Travel down to the base of the straight line and then continue in a curvy line that loops and meanders away from your note.

You can fill a whole area with just this one note and meanders, or you can challenge yourself to draw more musical notes and symbols with a continuous line and insert them into the design.

2 SCALY FISH: Make a simple fish shape, starting at the left side of the paper. Form an upward facing scallop shape, about 4″ from point to point. Continue the line, slanting below the scallop at an angle for about 1″ to start your fish's tail.

Draw a vertical line upward. And then draw a downward slanting line back to the end point of the scallop shape to finish your tail. Draw a downward-facing scallop, mirroring the first scallop and ending when the line meets your start point. Draw a curved line inside your fish to indicate a head, adding a loop for an eye.

Draw a series of small, vertical scales, filling the area inside the fish's body.

Travel around the fish's tail and then draw a wavy line to represent water, continuing across the page, from left to right. Stop and add another fish when you're ready.

When you reach the right side of the paper, travel down about ½″ and then echo the wavy line from the right side of the paper to the left. When you meet up with a fish, use the outside lines of the fish to travel. Continue echoing back and forth and adding fish into your design as you see fit.

Coaching

Doodle Launch Pad

Don't get derailed from completing the Daily Design Challenge by something as simple as not having a good pen around when you need it. If you haven't already, create a "doodle launchpad" for yourself. Gather your materials and put everything in one convenient place for the duration of the challenge. Your launch pad should be a place where you can easily store your materials and where you can stay comfortable but alert.

Small obstacles can keep us from realizing even our best intentions. On the other hand, small things and small actions can also give us the momentum we need to break free from what's holding us back. Isn't it worth it to do the small things that could give you an edge? Setting up your doodle launchpad is one action that could make the difference between finishing and giving up.

DAY 14: RECTANGLES

Prompt

We often think of quilts as being composed of squares or blocks. We may not realize how often rectangles feature in our quilts. They often go by other names, such as "piano keys" or "sashing."

When you're thinking of ways to fill up all the rectangle shapes inside your quilts, what could be more easy or natural than filling them with smaller rectangles? The rectangles inside become an echo of their outer container. We free-motion quilters know how pleasing an echo can be!

Rectangles are another geometric shape that often works well for modern quilts. A rectangle is a simple and flexible shape—much more adaptable than a square. You can stretch out a rectangle as long as necessary to fill a narrow, long space.

Technical Assistance

A rectangle, like any geometric shape, follows some rules. Rectangles have four sides and four 90° angles. The sides opposite each other must be parallel and equal in length.

Keep these rules in mind. If you're quilting a loose, whimsical looking quilt, it may not matter if your rectangles look a little wonky. If you think your quilt design calls for a clean, precise look, however, take more care when you form the corners and the sides of your rectangles. In cases when accuracy matters, use a ruler.

If you want to doodle with a ruler, an acrylic drafting ruler is a good option. The experience is going to be a bit different, however. Remember that when you draw a line with a pen, the pen marks right next to the edge of the ruler. When you quilt with a ruler and a ruler foot, the stitch line is ¼″ away from the edge of the ruler. You'll need to make that mental adjustment when you switch from one to the other.

Applications

1 **RECTANGLE TANGLE FILL:** This design is very similar to the Day 10 application 2. Triangle Tangle (page 44). You're just creating it with rectangles instead of triangles. Again, start by drawing a straight line from your border into the area you want to fill. After you've gone 2″–3″, draw a rectangle.

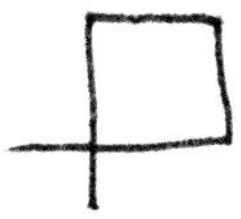

Travel away from the rectangle with either a straight line or a line that meanders a bit with occasional angles. For this design, don't let your meander line cross itself. Draw more rectangles periodically. Vary the sizes of the rectangles and try to space them evenly throughout the area you are filling.

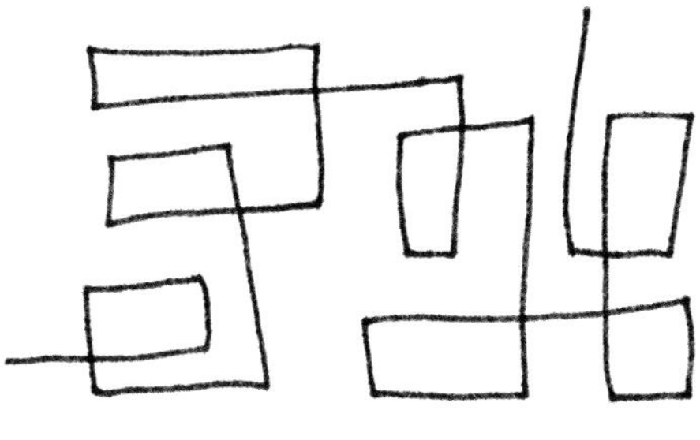

---

2 **INTERLOCKING RECTANGLES FILL:** Start by drawing a rectangle, oriented in any direction. Then travel a little along the first line of the rectangle and then pause. From this point, draw another rectangle that overlaps or "interlocks" with your first rectangle.

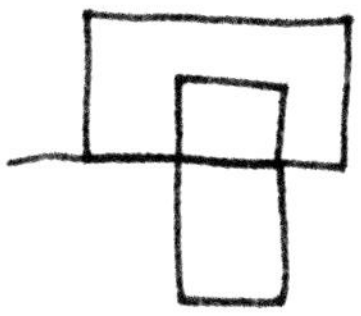

Continue drawing interlocking rectangles in this way. You can use any lines you have previously drawn to travel to areas that need to be filled. Vary the sizes and orientations of the rectangles and try to fill the areas evenly. Try not to draw your rectangles really close and make them small in one area while making them large and loose in another. You might need to practice a bit to get your scale and spacing even.

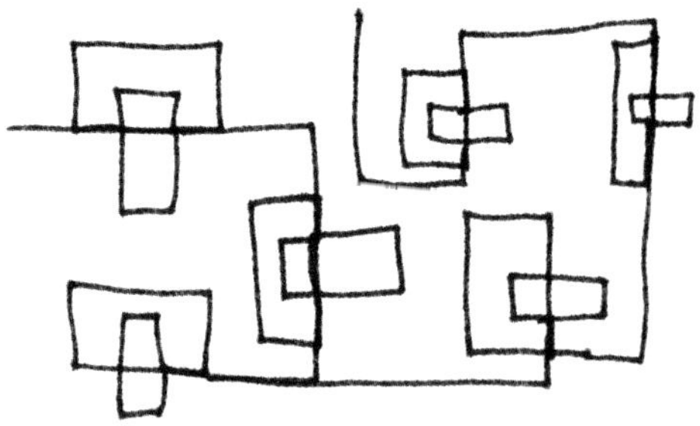

---

3 RECTANGLES ON A WIRE: This design works well for sashing and borders but it can also be stacked for filling larger areas. These rectangles are a little wonky on purpose. Imagine that you are filling a skinny sashing. You can draw guidelines horizontally across your page, if you like. Start a line, traveling from left to right, horizontally. When your line is about 2″ long, pause, then draw the first half of a rectangle by traveling up about ½″, then horizontally from right to left and then vertically down, crossing and stopping when you are about ½″ below your original line.

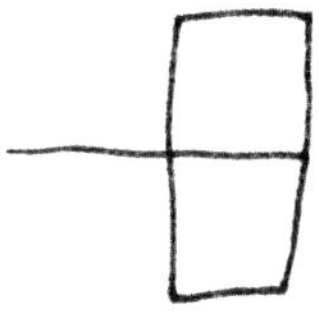

Complete the first rectangle by traveling horizontally from left to right and then up to meet the lower right corner of the first half of the rectangle.

To doodle a row, travel horizontally, from left to right again and repeat the steps above, this time drawing the lower half of the rectangle first. Because you're going for a wonky look, don't bother using a ruler for this. In fact, try to keep your lines loose and a little off-kilter and even round some of the corners.

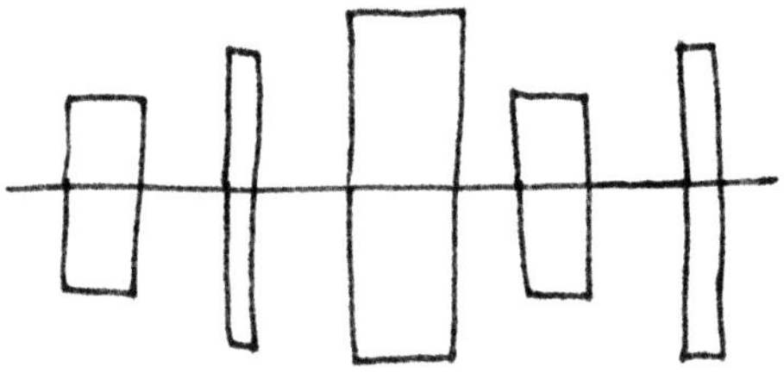

If you want to fill a large area with this design, you could work in several more rows below the first row by traveling down borders and alternating the direction you travel for each row.

Coaching

Building Habits

There are habits we want to make and habits we want to break. Creating a new habit can often feel like an elusive and even impossible thing, especially when we're in the beginning stages.

For Doodle School, we're asking you to create a free-motion doodle per day for 31 days. If you simply complete the 31 days of doodles, you've done and learned so much. Why not keep the learning and the momentum going? Think beyond the end of this challenge. You are already well on your way to establishing a very good long-term habit. You've already set yourself up for success, if you want to continue. Just keep going.

DAY 15: CRISSCROSS

Prompt

Today's prompt, Crisscross, is open for interpretation. We'd like you to create designs with lines that cross over one another, or lines that appear to cross over each other. Aside from that, there really are no rules.

You've probably seen aerial views of highway intersections. These are great for inspiration. Also, try searching "optical illusions" online. You'll see some images that will leave you feeling awestruck—and a little dizzy. What's more, there's so much crissing and crossing in modern architecture you can look there for inspiration and never run out of new ideas. You'll have no problem finding inspiration for this one.

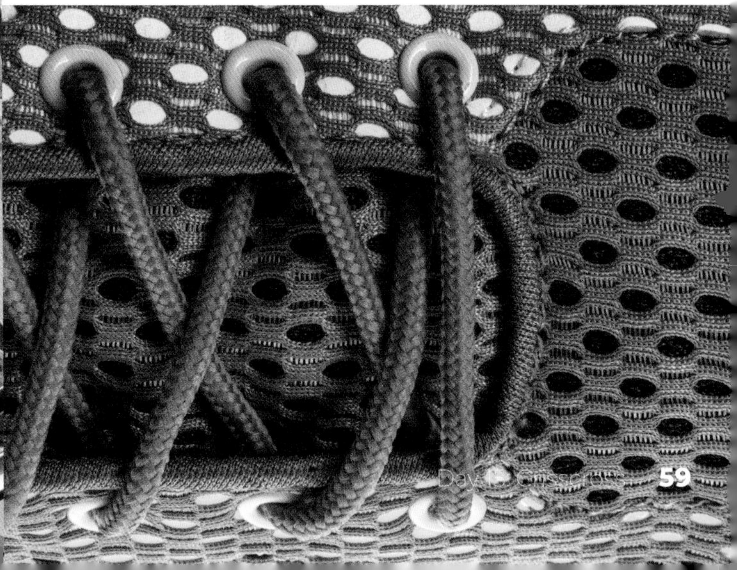

Technical Assistance

A grid isn't just a type of crisscross design, it's also a framework for creating other types of crisscross designs. If we turn a grid on its side, it becomes a grid that's "on point." Another term for that is *crosshatching*.

For today's prompt, use a sheet of graph paper. If you don't have graph paper, pull out that trusty ruler again and create your own grid. Using a grid to guide your doodles is very similar to marking a quilt top with a stencil.

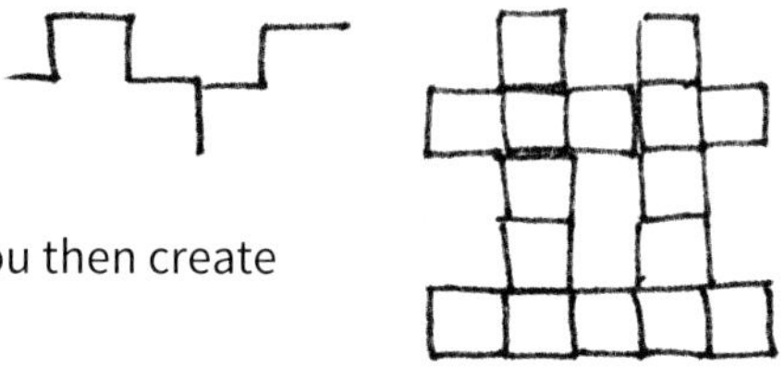

You can use the grid to create limitless designs (and not just crisscross designs, of course). You can easily create a continuous-line cross design in 2 passes by traveling across the grid once to create the tops of the crosses and once to create the bottoms of the crosses. You then create more rows in the same way, working back and forth as you go.

Applications

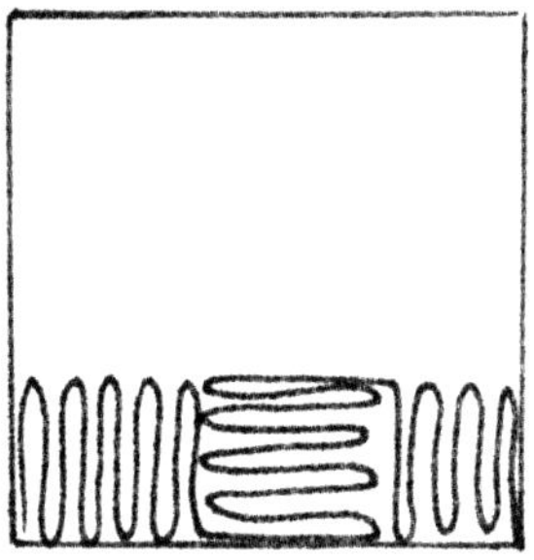

1 **BASKET WEAVE:** Create a grid of 2″ squares. In the first box of the grid, draw a series of vertical parallel lines, working from the left side of the box to the right. When your lines near the top and bottom of the box, use a sharp "U-turn" curve to turn around and continue in the reverse direction. Try to keep the spacing between your lines even.

When you reach the edge of the first box, fill the adjoining box with a series of horizontal parallel lines connected by U-turns. These lines should be spaced apart with the same spacing you used in the first box. You'll get good at this with practice.

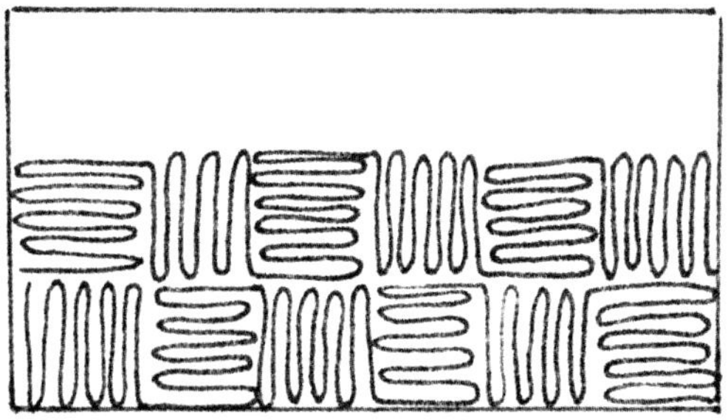

Continue across the first row in this manner, alternating the directions of your lines in each box, parallel and then horizontal. On the next row, work from the right to the left side of your page. Fill the first box with lines that are opposite from whatever you drew in the last box of the first line. If the box in the row below had horizontal lines, the first box in the second row should have vertical lines. Continue alternating the directions of the lines in the boxes, filling the space this way, row by row, right to left and then left to right.

2 CURVY X MARKS THE SPOT: This is a design Amy invented and one that she is "X-tra" fond of. Start by drawing a short, curvy line. We're going for a bold look here, so trace back and forth over this line 2–3 times, stopping in the center of the curve. Draw another curvy line across the middle of the first to form a curvy X. Go back and forth over the second curvy line, stopping somewhere near the end of this line. From there, draw a curvy line that crosses the tip of your last line just a bit and extends far enough away from the first X to give you room to form another X.

The third curvy line that you formed becomes half of the next X. Go over this third line 2–3 times, stopping at the center and then repeat the steps above to form another X. Again, draw a curvy line traveling away from the X and repeat. Keep doing this to fill your space.

Coaching

Vinyl Over Top of Quilt

When we try out a design on a quilt top without actually quilting it, we call it "auditioning" the design. One easy way to audition your design is to put a piece of clear vinyl on top of the quilt and draw on the vinyl with a dry erase marker. The clear vinyl we're thinking of is the type you might use as a table cover. You can often find it at fabric stores. An 18″ × 18″ square is a good size to start with—it can cover a large area, but it's still manageable.

You can audition multiple designs for your quilt with a piece of vinyl. If you want to remember and to compare your designs, take a picture of each before you clean the vinyl. After you've finished auditioning each design, *always* remove the vinyl from the top of the quilt before you wipe it clean. Take the vinyl to another area and clean it thoroughly before using it again. For easy storage, roll it up and keep it in a cool, dark place to prevent it from yellowing and becoming brittle.

DAY 16: VINES

Prompt

Vines can twist and turn along borders or meander through backgrounds. They give us lots of room for being creative. You can deck them out with leaves, flowers, or berries, or you can leave them bare.

When you get comfortable doodling vines, you'll probably notice they have a rhythm to them. Curve around, swing out, swing back; curve in the other direction, swing out, swing back, and so on. We think creating vines can be quite soothing … almost hypnotic. See what you think.

Technical Assistance

Start your vines at the center spine. The spine gives a vine its rhythm and its structure.

Vines can be organic and spontaneous like jazz music, which means you can make the spine curve back and forth as much as you like depending on where you want to go with it. You can also be spontaneous by periodically throwing in a leaf, a cluster of grapes, or something else.

Other times, you might want a more even look to your vines, more like a sonata. If you're putting a vine into a border, for example, and you want smooth, undulating curves along the center, you'll need to mark the center spine before you begin.

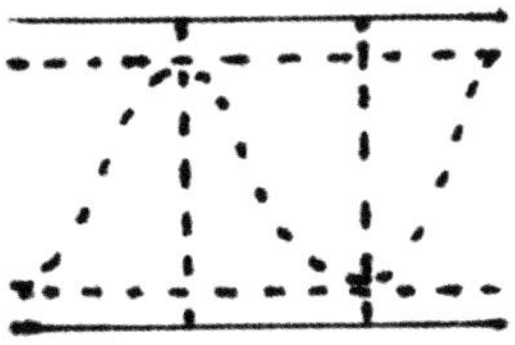

Draw 2 parallel horizontal guidelines across the paper. Make them about 4″ apart. Draw 2 dashed lines between and parallel to the guidelines. Divide the border into even sections, marking each section on the dotted lines. Starting from the left, draw a dotted S-curve in the first section, from the bottom dotted to the top dotted line. Continue drawing dotted S-curves in this way, alternating the direction of the curves from top to bottom and then bottom to top as you move from section to section. Remember to merge the curves with the dotted guidelines and not with the solid border guidelines. When you're finished making the S-curves, they should look a bit like a snake slithering between the guidelines. This curvy snake becomes the spine of the vine.

Once you've marked the dotted guideline for the spine, travel along it from left to right, adding leaves or other elements to either side. You can make your leaves even and regular along the spine, or you can create a bit of spontaneity by changing the sizes and positions of your leaves. Try throwing in some swirls, while you're at it.

Applications

1 PROPER AND BALANCED BORDER VINE: We've discussed creating an even spine, now let's learn one way of balancing the leaves on either side. Draw guidelines for your border and your spine, as you did in Technical Assistance (page 63).

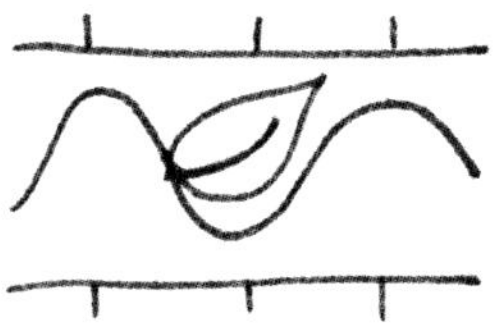

Working from the left side, draw a leaf shape in the first section. The bottom of the leaf should start at the bottom dotted line and the point should aim toward the top solid guideline. Draw a stem inside the leaf shape and pause at the base.

From the base of the leaf, trace the dotted spine guideline, stopping when you get to the next section. Draw another leaf on the opposite side of the vine, with its base at the top dotted guideline and its tip pointing toward the bottom solid guideline. Try to make the leaf equal in size and similar in shape to the first leaf. Continue in this way, following the spine and alternating leaves from side to side.

2 HEART-SHAPED LEAFY MEANDER VINE: Draw a 6″ square on the paper. Inside the square, from the left border, draw a swirl, in and then back out, on the same line. When you reach the base of the swirl draw a line that curves away from the swirl. At the end of the curve, draw a heart-shaped leaf.

From the base of the leaf, travel back along the curved line just a bit to form a stem. From there, draw a curved line that meanders a bit, traveling to an open area. Add more leaves and swirls to either side of the meandering line, traveling around until the area is filled.

3 **GRAPEVINE MEANDER:** Start as you did on the previous page, swirling in and then back out. Draw a curve away from the swirl. This time, to draw a grape leaf, make a series of jagged, zigzag lines that form 3 larger points.

When you reach the base of the leaf, travel inside the leaf and create a few branching veins. Travel along the center vein back to the base of the leaf. Follow the curved line a bit to create a stem, then use a curvy, loopy, line to travel to another area. Next, create another leaf but attach a bunch of grapes to it. Using the pebble technique from Day 2: Circles (page 15), draw a group of connected circles in a grape-cluster shape—larger at the top and narrower (1 or 2 grapes) at the tip.

Continue meandering with curves and loops. Throw some leaves, swirls, and grape clusters into the design when the mood hits you.

Coaching

Mixing Elements I

We think you're ready to start combining some of the designs you've learned. We recommend that you start with 3 simple designs that you've already mastered. For example, you might combine pebbles, rainbow swirls, and echoed leaves. Start by drawing each design in a cluster. Later, you can start to mix your designs together more. Continue to switch between the 3 designs and quilt them in clusters until your area is filled. Try to balance your 3 designs throughout the area. Don't quilt one section of leaves and forget to put any anywhere else.

DAY 17: FEATHERS

Prompt

Today, we're giving you options! You can choose to do one, two, or even all three of the following choices:

- Create traditional feathers, like the ones we demonstrate in Technical Assistance (next page).
- Learn one type of traditional free-motion feather and then create variations.
- Doodle something *like* a feather. Create your own style.

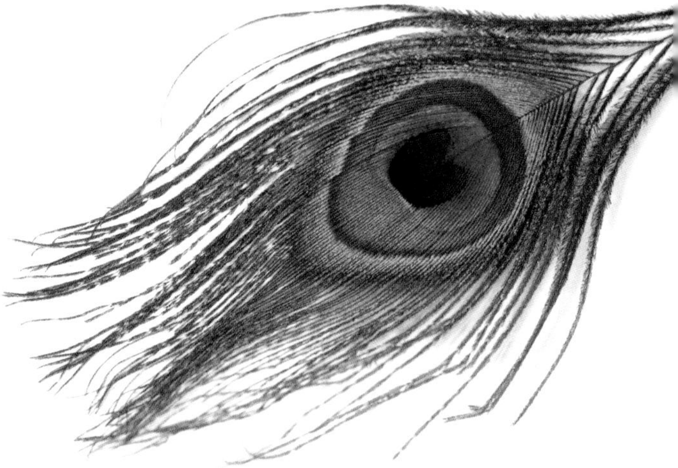

Technical Assistance

Let's start with a "bounce-back" feather. Make it with an implied spine, which means that you won't actually draw in a spine, instead mark a curvy, snake-like dotted guideline between 2 dotted guidelines in a border, as you did in Day 16's Technical Assistance (page 63). The curves of your dotted line do not need to be evenly spaced, but they can be. This snaky dotted line becomes your implied spine.

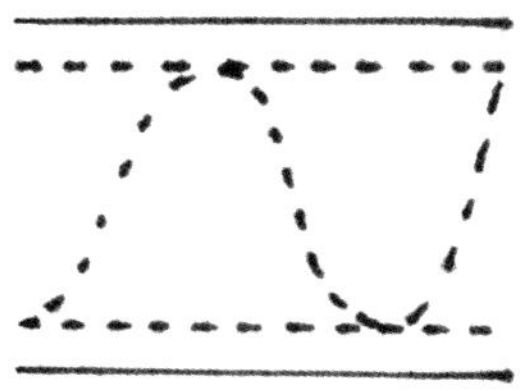

Draw 2 full plumes—one on each side of the implied spine. Draw the bottom plume first, reaching almost to the solid border guideline, and then arching up and back to the spine. When you come back to the implied spine at the center, imagine you are merging the line into the spine. Then, draw a plume above the spine guideline.

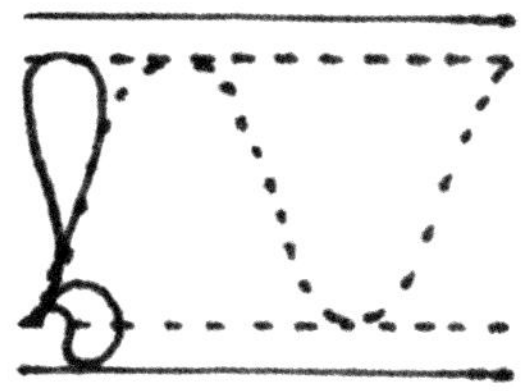

Form another plume below the spine guideline by drawing the top part of the plume and then curving down and to the left when you near the solid border guideline so that you merge into the top line of the previous plume.

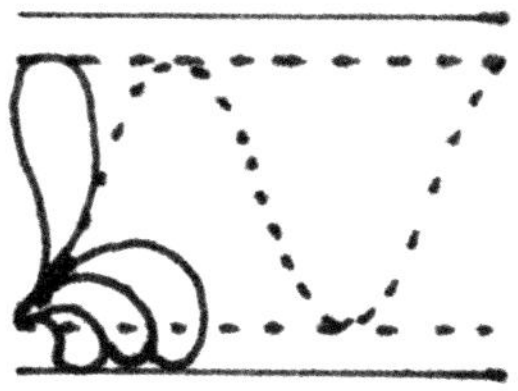

Reverse directions and trace back along the curve of the plume you just drew. Stop when you reach the top of the curve. Draw a line that breaks away from the plume and curves down again toward the solid lower border guideline. Just before you reach the guideline, curve sharply to the right and then up with a full curve that merges back with the spine and comes to rest just as it touches the previous plume in the spine.

You have just created 2 plumes beneath your spine guideline. Now, go above the spine and repeat. Continue to form plumes along the spine, moving from left to right inside your solid border guidelines. When you need to, you can vary the size of the plumes to fit the shape of your spine and the space you have available. Varying the sizes of your plumes can make your feathers more interesting.

Sometimes, you can curve the plume so that the top is really a part of the implied spine. Other times, you can create a smaller set of plumes when things are getting tight. There are times when you'll want to draw an extra set of plumes on one side to make it balance with the other side.

Applications

1 **BOUNCE-BACK FEATHER, ECHO VARIATION:** Begin as you did in Technical Assistance (page 67), drawing the same spine guideline between 2 border guidelines and creating a plume above and below the spine guideline. Then, draw the curved top of a feather under the spine guideline. This time, as you curve to meet the plume below, leave a bit of space between the curve of the plume and the bottom border guideline. Stop when your line meets the top of the first plume.

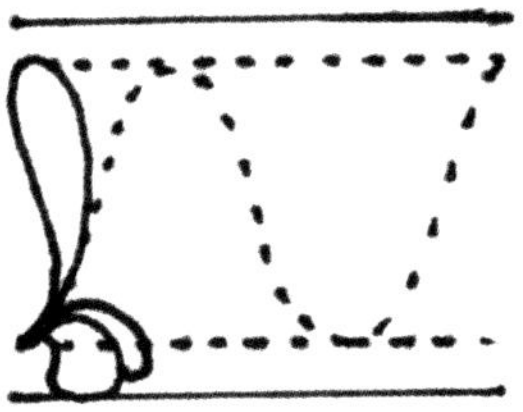

Instead of traveling back along the curve you just drew, draw a new curve that echoes closely, up and around the curve you just made. As you near the spine guideline, merge your echo line with the top of the curve below. Repeat on the top of the spine. Continue drawing echoed plumes above and below the spine guideline, alternating sides.

---

2 **FEATHER WITH A SPINE AND SEPARATE PLUMES:** Draw 2 solid horizontal guidelines about 5″ apart across the width of your paper. This time draw your spine between the 2 guidelines, with a slightly undulating solid line, starting at the left of the page and stopping at the right of the page.

For this design, you are going to draw all the plumes along the bottom of your spine before you move to the top. Start by drawing a plume on the bottom of the spine and then a second plume that closely follows the contour of the first plume. As you approach the solid border guideline, hook sharply upward and then curve back toward your spine. The base of your plumes should taper, so bring your curve gradually closer to the curve below as you approach the spine.

Bring the end of the curve close to the spine, but do not merge the curve with the spine. Create plumes all along the bottom of the spine. As you near the right side of the spine, decrease the sizes of the plumes and make the tops angle more steeply upward. When you make your last plume on the right side, merge the top of it with the spine.

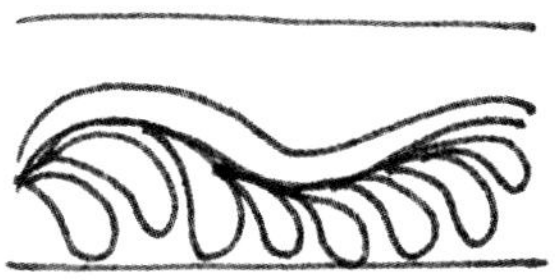

Draw the top of the spine by echoing your first spine guideline from the right of the page to the left. Draw plumes along the top of the feather. Merge your last plume with the spine. Travel back to the left side of the feather by filing the spine with a string of pebbles. Echo the entire feather.

Coaching

What's Your Greatest Takeaway?

Out of all the things you've learned so far, what would you say is your greatest takeaway? Write it down on a note card and put it up somewhere where you can see it every day, for the rest of the challenge. Your key takeaway says something special about you. It says that you're willing to invest in your own learning and growth. It says that you can work hard at something. It tells you you're progressing. It tells you that there is still so much you can learn and do in this life. Reread your card often. It will motivate you to keep going and see this challenge through to the end.

DAY 18: CLAMSHELLS

Prompt

Do you know what we mean when we talk about clamshells in the quilting world? Well … they look exactly like fish scales. Somewhere along the line, someone decided they looked like rows of clamshells all lined up. So, we don't call them fish scales, we call them clamshells. Maybe the difference is in the, *ahem* … scale?

Clamshells are usually large enough that you can decorate their insides, which is quite convenient, since it is so much fun to do just that. In addition, there are numerous ways to create variety in clamshells, even without putting patterns inside them. Think about how simply changing the height of the clamshells or the width changes the look so completely. We think you're going to love clamshells as much as we do.

Technical Assistance

Making a section of clamshells couldn't be easier. Start at the bottom left of the paper. Draw a row of scallop shapes from left to right, horizontally across your page. Practice keeping them a consistent height and width. If you struggle with this, draw a grid to guide you. Make each of the scallops the size of 1 box in the grid.

When you get to the edge of the paper, travel up and begin the next row, working from right to left. The scallops in the second row should be staggered, so that their bases connect with the centers of the peaks of the scallops below.

Once you feel comfortable with drawing clamshells, try drawing them in various sizes and keeping them consistent within each size. Make a section of short and wide ones and a section of tall and narrow ones. Can you think of any other ways to alter the size or shape of your clamshells?

Next, draw a section of echoed clamshells. Echo each row before you travel up to the next row.

While you're at it, why not draw some more rows of clamshells and echo them twice? Just look at all the clamshell variations you can create!

Applications

1 **CLAMSHELL SPROUTS:** Let's get busy decorating the insides of your clamshells! Draw your first scallop, traveling from left to right. Before you begin the second scallop, draw 3 small teardrop-shape leaves. Draw the leaf in the middle first, then smaller, slightly curved leaves on each side.

Draw your second scallop and a second set of leaves. Continue in this manner, across the page, and then travel up and draw another row of scallops and sprouts, moving from right to left. Continue until you have doodled several rows.

2 ORANGE SLICE CLAMSHELLS: Again, start by drawing 1 scallop, traveling from left to right across the paper. Next, draw 3 wedge shapes, starting with a tall wedge in the center, then a smaller, slightly curved wedge shape to either side of the first.

Continue in this manner, alternating between scallops and wedges, to fill your first row. You will form the rest of the rows in the same way. When you draw the scallops, their arches will echo the 3 wedge shapes from the row beneath.

3 FEATHERED CLAMSHELLS: Draw 1 scallop. Draw the design inside the scallop, instead of to the right of the scallop. Traveling to your left and into the scallop, draw 1 small feather plume and then 2 larger feather plumes over that. The largest plume should echo the inside curve of the scallop.

Fill the first row in this manner and then travel up and draw another row traveling from right to left. Draw several rows for practice.

4 **CLAMSHELL CLOUDS:** By making a small change to the outline of your scallops, you're going to make clamshells that look like a sky full of clouds. To form your first scallop, start to draw your curve as you normally would. Before you reach the peak of your scallop, draw a small bump.

Next, draw another, larger bump that reaches up to the peak of your scallop and then back down, stopping directly across from where it started. Make another small bump to the right of this bump, continuing your line until it reaches the base of your clamshell, across from its starting point.

Fill in an entire area with several rows of cloud bumps to get the cloudy sky effect.

Coaching

Mixing Elements II

Are you ready to mix things up a little more? This time, use slightly more difficult designs, mix your designs together more, and add in some echoing. Try combining a curved feather with a spine, a swirl hook, echoed hearts, and pebbles.

This time you aren't forming clusters, so don't put more than three or four of the same shape together. If you're filling in a large area, look ahead to see where you can fit another feather or two. When you get to these areas, put your feathers in first. You might find it helpful to mark guidelines for placing the spines of your feathers before you begin your design.

DAY 19: SHADOWS

Prompt

Shadow is a word (like *scale*) that has multiple meanings. If we use it as a noun, it's usually a dark outline created on a surface when an object blocks light from hitting that surface. As a verb, *to shadow* can mean to closely follow something or someone. We could go on, but we think these two meanings suit our purposes. So, how can we apply shadow(s) to free-motion quilting? Read on.

Technical Assistance

Whenever you quilt, you're most likely defining and creating shadowed areas and highlighted areas in your quilts. Think about it—the quilted areas are thrown into shadow and the unquilted areas pop up into the light.

Are you familiar with trapunto quilting? Take a minute to search it online, if you aren't. Trapunto takes full advantage of this light-bending superpower we quilters have.

So, how can you use this ability for today's prompt? If you want to throw something—a shape, maybe—into shadow, quilt it more heavily. If you want something to pop, leave it unquilted or lightly quilted and quilt the area around it more heavily.

Consider how you can apply the verb "to shadow" in quilting. In Day 1: Lines (page 12), we talked about ways you can create patterns by alternating the spacing between your lines. Try doing this with a series of echoes.

Draw 2 echoes close to each other and 2 far apart. Repeat this pattern and then look at what you've got. It looks like the second of the close-together echoes is "shadowing" the first. Every time you put 2 close-together echoes into the design, you create a shadowing effect that ripples outward.

Applications

1 **SHADOW WAVES:** Let's use the verb definition of shadow to create a wavy effect, like sandstone in a desert. Starting at the edge of your paper, draw a gently waving line back to the border of your paper.

Closely echo all the way around the first line. Travel along the border a little, then create another echo that is farther away. Continue a few more times in this pattern: close, far; close, far; close, far.

Travel along the border of your paper to another area. Draw another wavy line and repeat the same echo pattern around this wavy line. When your lines intersect with the outer echo from the previous area, travel along the outer echo in the same way you would the border of the paper.

Continue to echo your current pattern a few more times. Travel to a third area and repeat until you have filled the space.

---

2 **SHADOWY DISKS:** Start big with this one. Draw a crescent shape and then echo the crescent shape 4 times. Each time your echoes should merge at the base of the first crescent.

Travel into the space between the original crescent and the first echo and fill this space with close matchstick lines. When this space is filled, travel to the space between the third echo and the fourth echo and fill this space with matchstick lines.

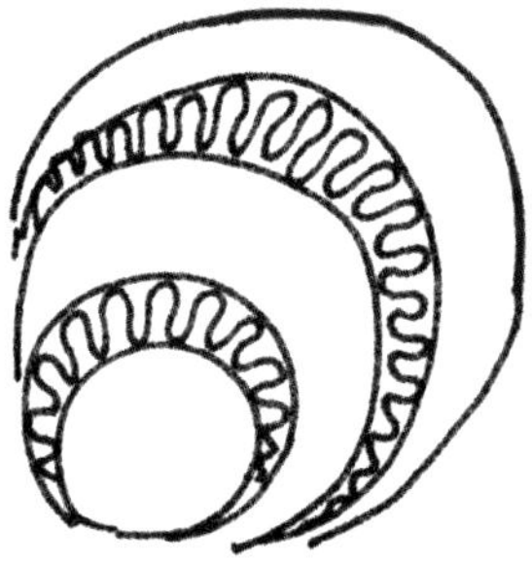

Travel along the outside of the last echo to an open space and draw a new crescent that connects to the outside border of your first shadowy disk on both ends.

Complete a second set of shadowy discs in the same manner as the first. Repeat. When you create new crescents, you can echo them more than 4 times, as long as you echo them an even number of times. An even number of echoes keeps your shadows consistent.

3 **SPOOKY GHOST FILL:** You've probably drawn some ghost shapes around Halloween. So, now, let's give your ghosts some shadows to make then creepier. Draw a ghost shape, starting with the head.

After you close the ghost shape at the head, travel into the head area with a short line and draw 3 circles for the eyes and mouth. Draw the circles right next to each other or connect them with short travel lines. You can black out the eyes and mouth with zigzag lines before moving on, if you want. Use the line you created traveling into the head to travel back out to the edge of the ghost. Draw an echo around the right side of your ghost, from the top of its head to the bottom of its "sheet" on the right side. Fill the space between your ghost and its echo with diagonal lines.

Travel to another area using windy-looking swirls and then doodle another ghost in the same way. Try adding some bats with shadows and, maybe, a moon—if you're feeling brave.

Coaching

Building Stamina

If you doodle too long and press down hard on your pen without stopping, you could get a hand cramp. If you quilt without stopping periodically, your shoulders, wrists, back, and even your neck might start complaining. Free-motion quilting uses repetitive motions that can inflame your joints and cause long-term damage, if you're not careful.

So, as you're building endurance for free-motion quilting, you're never going to be working toward marathon quilting sessions. Your goal should be enough stamina to quilt for a reasonable amount of time—maybe a half-hour to an hour, tops. And when you've reached your goal? Stop. Take a good break—at least fifteen minutes. When you take a break, stretch your shoulders and your wrists and your neck, just like any good athlete in training would.

DAY 20: WALLS

Prompt

What associations do you make when you think of walls?

For Dara, so many crazy ideas come to mind. She thinks about the Berlin Wall, about Pink Floyd's song, about ancient runes, about how walls keep her safe, different heights of walls, textures of walls. . . .

The first place Amy's mind goes to is the things walls can be made of—and there are so many things! Walls can be made of bricks, round stones, rough stones, stucco, plaster, cinder blocks. . . . They also can be covered with interesting things, such as wood planks, shingles, bead-board, ivy, moss, paintings, tiles, quilts (yay!), tapestries, wallpaper, graffiti, shelves of knickknacks. . . .

What do you think of?

Technical Assistance

Let's create a simple brick wall. Grab a ruler and draw a 4″ square on your paper. Inside the square, draw several horizontal, evenly spaced, dotted guidelines. The guidelines should be about ½″ apart and touch the borders of your square on the left and right sides.

Working from left to right, trace along the bottom horizontal dotted guideline for about 1″. From this point, draw a vertical line down to the bottom border of the square. Then trace the vertical line back up to the first horizontal guideline. Continue traveling left to right along this guideline, drawing vertical lines down to the bottom border of the square and back up to the guideline at 1″ intervals.

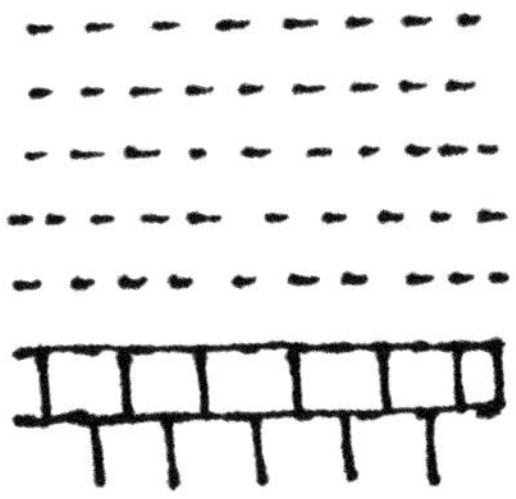

When you reach the right side of the square, travel up the border to the second horizontal guideline. Trace across the second guideline from right to left. You want this row of bricks to be staggered over the first row. To accomplish this, make the first brick in this row half-size by drawing the first vertical line about ½″ from the right margin. Draw this vertical line, down to the first guideline and then back up to the second one. Continue across this row, drawing vertical lines between the guidelines at 1″ intervals. End the second row with another half-size brick.

Continue in this manner until you've filled the square with bricks. Be sure to line up all the vertical lines in odd rows with each other and the vertical lines in even rows with each other.

Applications

1 **OLD BRICK WALL:** For a rustic brick wall, your bricks can vary a little in size and your rows don't need to be perfectly straight. Build each row upon the last, keeping it as straight as possible but not worrying about getting it perfect.

Start by drawing another 4″ square on your paper and don't draw any dotted guidelines. You want your finished brick wall to look a little rough and wonky. Your finished bricks should be rectangular, but slightly rounded at the corners. You'll also want a little space between the bricks, to look like mortar.

For the first row, travel ½″ up the left border of the square and draw a 1⅛″ horizontal line, from left to right, inside the square. Then travel down to about ⅛″ above the bottom border and draw, from right to left, a line parallel with the bottom of the square, stopping about ⅛″ away from the left edge of the square. Travel up, echoing the left edge of the square until you meet the top line of the first brick. Trace across the top line of the brick until you reach the upper right rounded corner of the brick. Continue this line horizontally about ⅛″ beyond the upper right corner of your first brick.

Make the second brick in the same manner as the first but this time, travel in a counterclockwise direction. Leaving about ⅛″ gap between the right edge of the first brick and the left edge of the second brick, draw a line down to about ⅛″ above the bottom edge of the square. Traveling horizontally, from left to right, draw the bottom edge of the second brick about 1″ across. Travel up until the right side of the second brick is roughly the same height as the first brick. Travel horizontally from right to left until you reach the left side of the second brick. (This will be the vertical line you drew ⅛″ to the right of your first brick.) Trace up the left side of the second brick and then from left to right along the top to about ⅛″ from the right of the second brick.

Complete your remaining bricks in this manner—create all odd bricks by traveling clockwise and all even bricks by traveling counterclockwise. The final brick might not be 1″ across. That's okay.

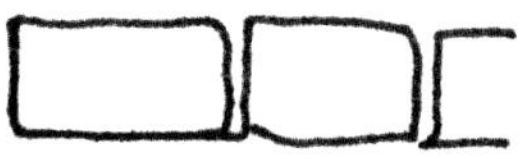

Travel up, echoing the right margin of the square. Stop at about ⅛″ above the first row of bricks. Start the first brick on the second row by traveling horizontally, right to left. When you reach the midpoint of the last brick in row one, change directions and begin to travel vertically. Travel up about ½″ and then switch directions again and travel horizontally, from left to right, until you are about ⅛″ away from the right side of the square. Travel down to the lower right corner of the first brick in the second row. Trace the bottom edge of the first brick in the second row and then continue beyond the lower left corner of this brick about ⅛″.

Form the rest of the second row of bricks in the same manner as the first row, alternating the direction you travel (clockwise and then counterclockwise) with each brick. When you are near the left edge of the square, travel up and create a third row of bricks. Roughly line up the gaps between the bricks in the third row with the gaps between the bricks in the first row. When the third row is complete, travel up to about ⅛″ above the third row and create a fourth row of bricks, lining up the gaps in this row with the gaps in the second row. Fill in the entire square in this manner.

2 **STONE WALL:** It's easy to create a stone wall by varying the size and shape of the stones. You can include space (for mortar) between the stones, if you want.

Draw another 4″ square. Starting inside the lower left corner of the square, use a figure-eight motion to form the first 2 stones. Instead of creating 2 circles or 2 rounded rectangles, make irregular shapes that resemble stones. Occasionally, throw in a stone that is quite a bit taller than the rest.

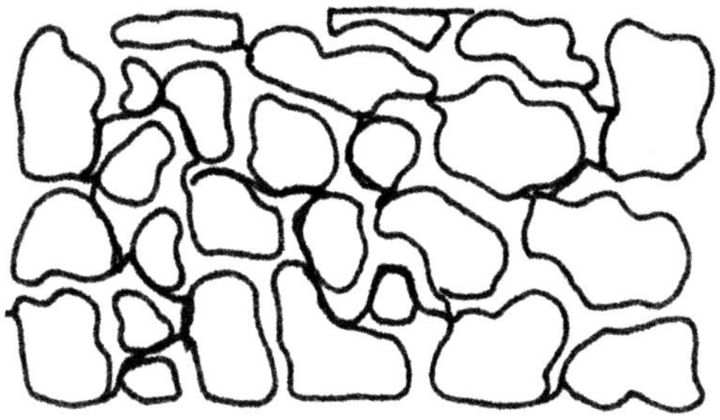

Form the second row by traveling up the right margin of the square and working from right to left. Again, occasionally draw in a larger, taller stone. When you reach a large stone from the previous row, travel up the side of the larger stone (or echo if you're going for a mortar look). Reverse the direction you are traveling. Go backward and create a third row of stones that brings the shorter rows of stones up to the level of the large stone. Whenever you run into a large stone, work in a row or two, traveling back and forth, to fill in the gaps between large stones.

Coaching

Compound Effect

Are you familiar with a "compound effect?" It's the idea that from small, consistent actions, we reap huge rewards in time. Some things just have to be built over time. The good news is that building free-motion skills over time is pretty painless.

Drawing a continuous-line doodle a day is a pretty small thing, right? Compared to beautifully quilting a queen-size quilt, it's a piece of cake. Keep doodling and practicing consistently, however, and you will be able to quilt stunning queen-size quilts in time.

Dara loves this quote from Abraham Lincoln, "The best way to predict the future is to create it." We think the easiest way to predict the future is to start creating it through small, consistent actions starting today. You're already on the right track because you're participating in Doodle School. Keep going. Future you and your future quilts are going to be even better than you imagine.

DAY 21: WATER

Prompt

Think about the movement of water. How does water flow? Take a look at as many water images as you can in books or online. Look at water in art and see how artists depict it. See if you notice anything that you've never noticed about water before.

Where do we find water? It's in lakes, rivers, oceans, streams, puddles, mugs, glasses, pots, baths, bird baths, raindrops, windowpanes. . . . Have we missed any places? We're sure you can think of more.

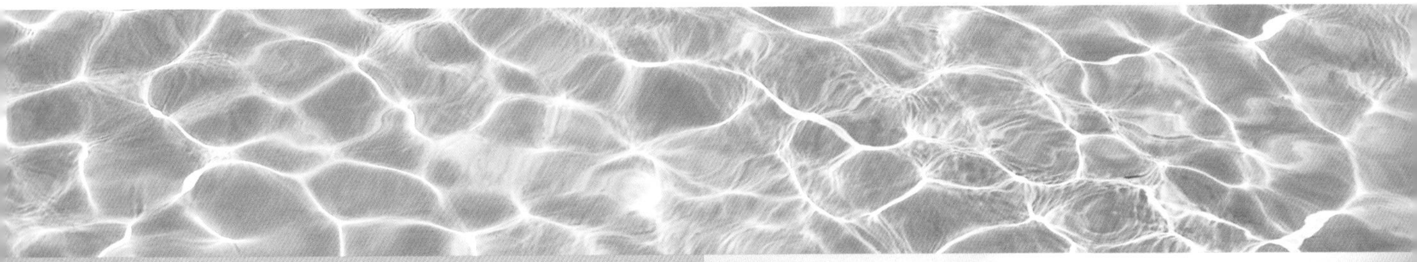

Technical Assistance

Dara once quilted a quilt that depicted all the provinces in Canada. Many of the areas had water in them and she quilted the water differently in each one. Water can take so many shapes and forms.

Still water can look glassy with perceptible ripples. Quilt lightly, with only a few slightly wavy lines. If anything drops into a quiet pond, the effects are very noticeable. You'll see clear ripples emanating from the spot where the water was disturbed. So, you might want to include some ripples, here and there.

When water flows slowly and gently, you'll see deeper waves and more wavy lines. If the water flows around something, such as a rock, it parts around the rock and often flows back together on the other side. You'll also see more bubbles around rocks or anything that disturbs the water.

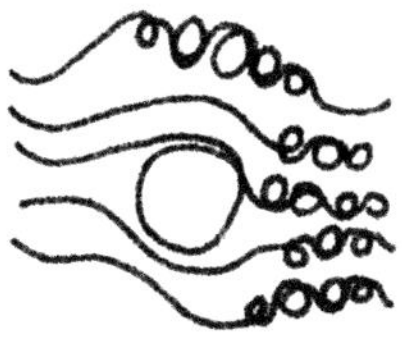

What about forceful water? The lines where there is the strongest force in the water are straight and bold.

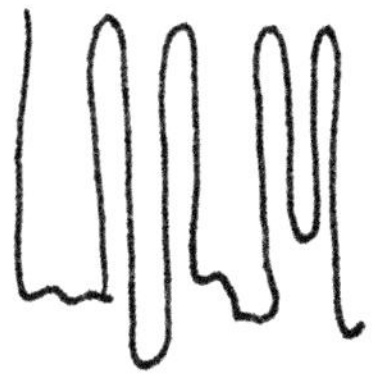

When the force of flowing water hits the water in the pool or tub below, there is a lot of bubbling and splashing. Add some splashes and bubbling to your design.

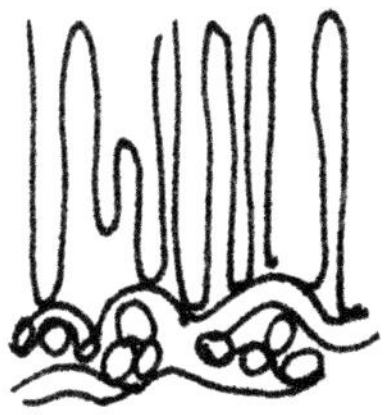

Applications

1 SWIRLY WAVES FILL: Start by drawing a horizontal S-curve from left to right across the paper. The first part of the curve swoops down and is somewhat long and then swoops up and around into a smaller curve and then a spiral.

To continue, spiral out of the swirl, echoing the inside of the curve. Instead of echoing all the way around the spiral, echo the long swoop of the first part of the S-curve and merge with the curve at the tip.

Then, echo the top of the S-curve traveling around the spiral and merging your line with the previous echo line. From this point, form the first part of the S-curve of the next wave.

Repeat the steps from the first wave to form a second wave and continue in this way across the paper.

Travel up the border and form another row of waves. Stagger the placement of the swirls in this row so that they don't line up exactly with the swirls in the row beneath. You can orient the waves in the second row the same direction as in the first row by making a mental adjustment and drawing the spiral of the wave first or you can simply flip the direction of these waves so that they travel from right to left.

---

2 GENTLE POND WATER FILL: Draw a 4″ square. Draw an S-curve that starts at the bottom left border of the square and ends at the bottom right border. Your curves should be gentle, not deep.

Travel up the right margin of the square, a bit. Form an S-curve, moving from right to left. Your line can curve and flow, up and down, more than once. At some point, merge this second S-curve with one of the lines from the row below. Next, reverse the direction you are traveling and draw an S-curve moving from left to right again. This line should echo the curves of the line directly below it, until you reach the right margin again.

Make the next S-curve moving from right to left again. When you need to, swoop down at a steeper angle to echo the curves of the first row. Continue to the left margin. Continue working back and forth inside the square, occasionally merging your line with the line below it and then reversing direction and traveling back the way you came. If you develop an especially deep curve somewhere, you can fill it in by echoing back and forth between the steep curve and the opposite margin of the square, until you reach the top of the steep curve.

Coaching

Creating Your Own Designs

Have you started creating some of your own continuous-line designs yet? If not, we're not judging you. If you feel ready to try, however, we'd like to provide some guidance.

Find a picture of the thing you want to make into a continuous-line design and print it out. Place tracing paper or a thin paper, such as copy paper, over your picture.

Tape your papers to a lightbox, a lit tablet, a sunny window, or a glass coffee table. If you use a coffee table, shine a light behind your papers to see the outline of your picture more clearly.

Think about the simplest way to trace your picture with a continuous line. Trace your image, following the path you determined. Did it work? Now that you've tried it, can you think of an easier way? If you think you could make it easier or better, try again.

You've created your own design! Simple, right?

DAY 22: REPEAT

Prompt

What do you think is the difference between repeat and echo?

An *echo* is defined as a sound or series of sounds caused by the reflection of sound waves from a surface back to the listener. "The walls threw back the echoes of his footsteps."

A *repeat* is defined as saying something again that has been said or doing the same action as someone else.

These definitions generate a lot of ideas for us—what about you?

Technical Assistance

What do you get when you repeat a design? One of our favorite things is a repeat pattern. You can take any of the designs you've already learned and repeat it in an organized way to create a pattern.

So, what do we mean by "repeat it in an organized way"? Possibly the simplest way to do this is to repeat your design in horizontal or vertical lines. You can also easily repeat a pattern in an organized way by placing it into a grid. Your grid doesn't have to be made of squares, either. Your grid could be made from other geometric shapes, such as hexagons. The purpose of the grids is to give you guidelines for repeating your design and creating your pattern. (See the application 2. Divide and Conquer, page 88.)

A good example of a repeat pattern is a mandala. If you look at a mandala, it's made up of equal-size, pie-shape sections that each repeat the same pattern. You can easily create a balanced mandala by using a pencil to mark out a circle with horizontal and vertical lines crossing at its center and then diagonal lines crossing the center at 45° angles.

Next, think of a design you know that can travel in a repeat pattern around a circle. Draw this design around the center of your circle, using the guidelines to keep it evenly spaced and equal in size.

Think of another design and repeat it around the previous design, keeping it evenly sized and equally spaced. Continue to add repeat layers around the previous designs until your circle is full.

Applications

1 **COILS:** Let's start with a simple repeat design. Start at the top left of the paper and draw loopy coils in a vertical row down the page.

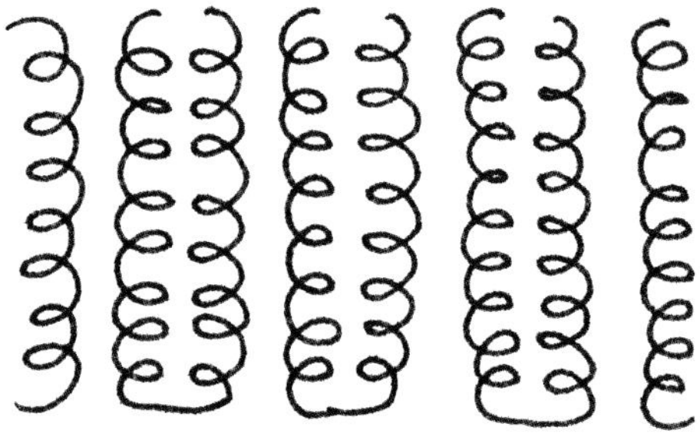

For the next row, travel along the bottom margin and then draw another row of loopy coils traveling up the page. This time flip your coils so that the loops are on the opposite side from your first row.

Continue drawing coils up and down the page, alternating the direction of the coils each time.

2 **DIVIDE AND CONQUER:** Here's an example of a repeat pattern created using a grid. Draw a grid on your paper with 1½″ squares. You are going to create each row in 2 passes. On the first pass, divide each square diagonally. Start at the lower left corner of the first square on the left and draw a diagonal line to the upper right corner of the square. In the next square, continue the line, drawing from the upper left corner to the lower right corner of the second square. Repeat in this manner across the entire row of squares.

Travel up the right margin to the next row. In this row, draw a diagonal line at an opposite angle to the box below. If the box below is divided by a diagonal line that slants up from the lower right, the diagonal line in the box you are about to divide should start at the upper right corner and travel to the lower left corner of the box, and so on. Each time you divide a box, reverse the angle, working from right to left. When you reach the left margin, travel up the margin and divide the third row in the same manner as the first row. At the end of the third row, travel up your right margin and then divide the fourth row in the same manner as your second row. All the dividing lines in odd rows should slant in the same directions and all the dividing lines in even rows should slant in the same directions.

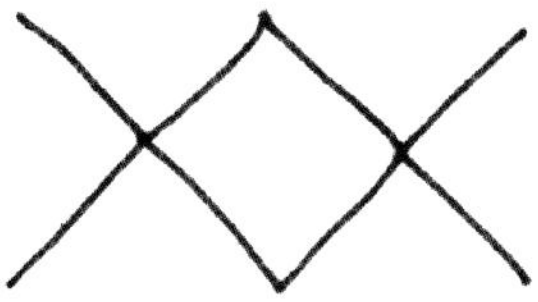

Then, travel into the triangle closest to where you finished dividing up the boxes of the grid. Fill the triangle with a series of horizontal matchstick lines. Travel to the adjacent triangle in the same box and fill it with a series of vertical matchstick lines. Continue to the closest triangle in the second box and fill it with horizontal matchstick lines. Continue in this way across the row, alternating between horizontal and vertical lines.

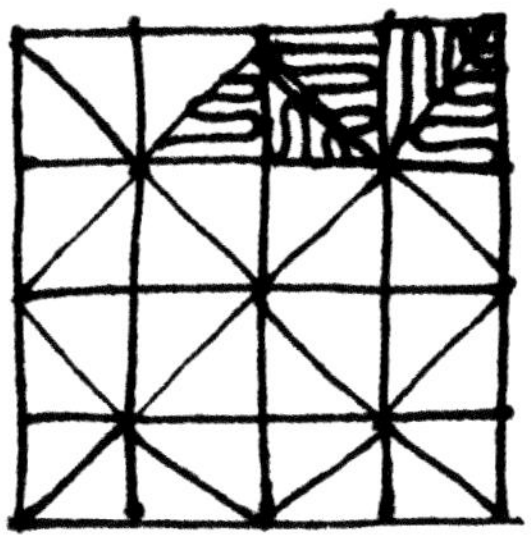

Travel down the margin to the next row. Fill the first triangle with vertical lines and the second with horizontal lines. Continue to alternate across the row following this pattern. Alternate the direction of the matchstick lines you begin with as you start each new row.

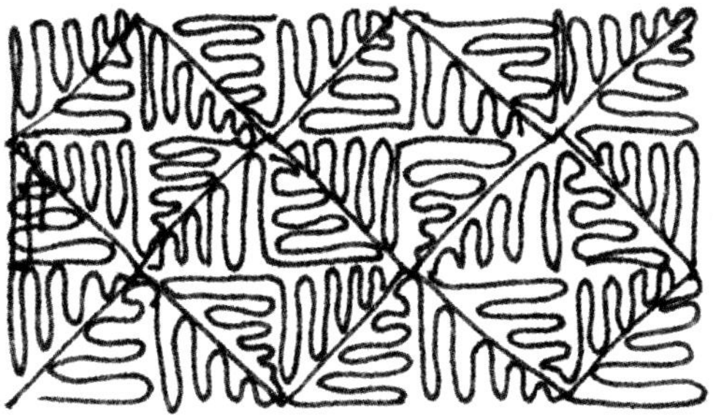

Coaching

Pick a Quilt

Are you nervous about taking your doodles from paper to quilt? Try this. Choose a simple quilt block—do a quick online search if you need ideas. Look for one that consists of simple geometric shapes, such as Churn Dash, Flying Geese, or Broken Dishes. Draft a simple quilt on paper that consists of four identical blocks with sashing in between. Color your quilt with light-colored markers, so that you can see the design easily. Finally, make two or three copies. In the next coaching session, we'll talk about planning and executing your design.

DAY 23: ROCKS AND PEBBLES

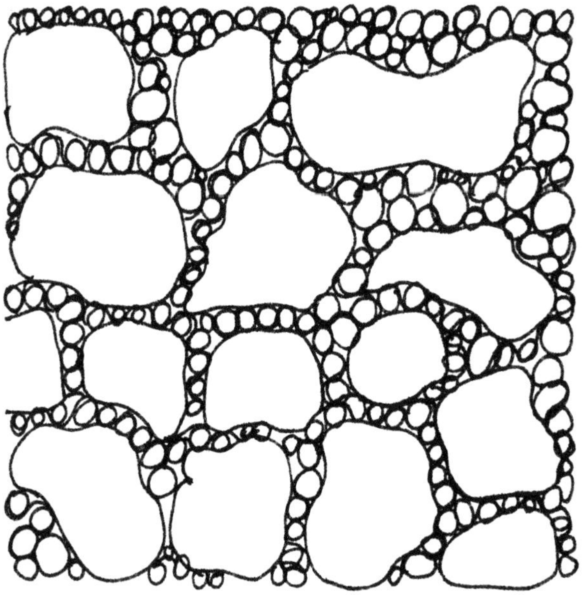

Prompt

In Day 2: Circles (page 15), you learned the technique for creating pebbles. In Day 20: Walls, application 2. Stone Wall (page 81), you doodled a rock wall. What else can you do with rocks and pebbles? Surprisingly, quite a lot.

As you create your designs, here are a few questions to get you started. What are the differences between rocks and pebbles? Where do you find them? How big are they? What color are they? Are they solid or spotted? What kinds of texture do they have?

Technical Assistance

First, we recommend you watch Dara's YouTube video "Dara Doodle Challenge Day 23." It's very helpful and you'll get to experience her fabulous teaching skills in action.

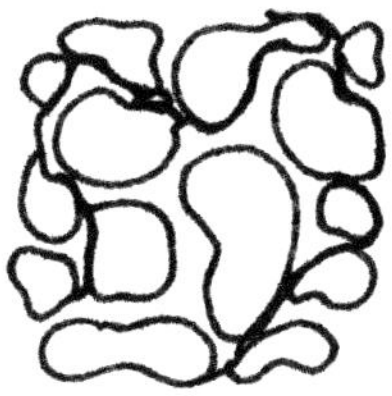

You can create a bunch of pebbles to fit any space by using a figure-eight motion and traveling around the outside of 1 pebble to get to the next one. Let's try making variations on traditional free-motion pebbling. First, vary the shapes of your pebbles. Make their edges irregular and sometimes wavy. Make some oblong and some squarish. Add in some sharp angles and make some flat, like shale.

Now, vary the sizes of your pebbles. Create river rocks with some large rocks and some medium rocks surrounded by lots of smaller pebbles. Quilt into your larger rocks and add some cracks or other texture.

Applications

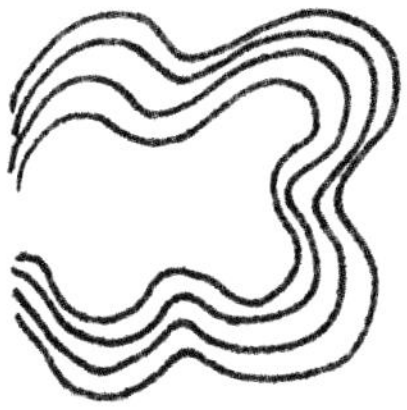

1 **SANDSTONE:** If you've ever been to a sandstone desert, you've probably seen the layers that are revealed in the rock through erosion. That's what this design reminds us of. Create the first rock so it looks wavy and flat. Echo closely around it several times.

Draw another rock that is connected to the outside echo of the first rock. Echo this rock several times, as well. Continue in this manner, using the outside echoes of the rocks to travel as necessary.

2 ZEN GARDEN: Mark a light, wavy guideline across your paper. Following your wavy line, create a trail of stones that are similar shape and size. Create a pattern with your stones, if you want.

Create a Zen pile of stones by drawing a large wavy circle with a smaller wavy circle inside it and a smaller wavy circle inside that, and so on. The outside edges of the circles can touch wherever you like. Travel out of your circles back to the curved line you drew to travel to this area. Travel out a bit on this line and then echo around your Zen rock pile.

When you reach your line again, travel out on it a bit more and echo again. Repeat this to fill up the area. This is meant to look like sand that has been combed around the pile.

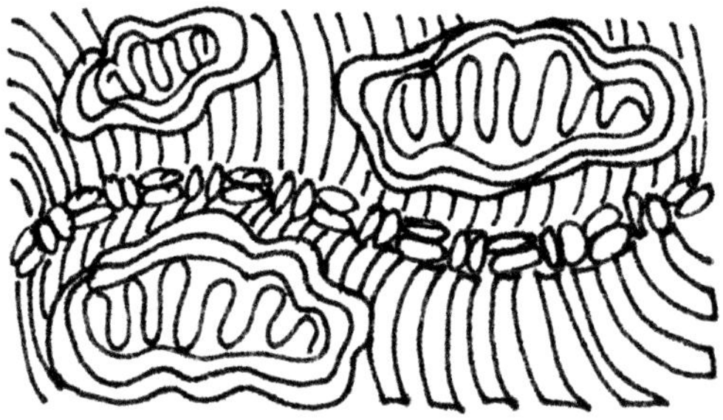

3 DECORATED PEBBLES: Begin doodling a cluster of pebbles using a roundish pebble design. Add some fairly large pebbles throughout. Whenever you draw a larger pebble, fill in the inside with a decoration. We've given you a few design ideas below.

- *For an asterisk:* Travel in a straight line across the center of the pebble. Reverse direction and travel back on the line to the center of the pebble. Draw another line that bisects the pebble and is perpendicular to the first line. Travel back and forth to make the line complete. Draw 2 more lines that crisscross the first 2 lines. Travel to the outside of the pebble and continue pebbling. Periodically throw asterisked pebbles into your design in a way that spreads them around the area.

- *For a flower:* Draw a small petal shape that ends at the center of the pebble. Travel back to the center of the pebble along the edge of the petal and then draw more petals radiating out from the center. Travel along a petal to get back to the outside of your pebble again.

- *To add spirals:* Simply spiral into the center of the pebbles and then back out on the same line. To create a swirl, travel into the center and then echo the spiral back to the outside of the pebble.

Coaching

Make a Plan

Let's audition some designs for the quilt you drafted in Day 22: Repeat (page 86). Choose four or more doodles you like and use them to fill in one of your copies. You may need to think about how you could fit the designs into triangles or into sashing. Also, think about the directions you want your designs to be oriented. Plan how you will travel from one area to another. If it helps you remember your travel path, draw small arrows in a different color from your marker. If you get stuck in a block, try backtracking along previous lines or your seams to travel to the next area.

Audition alternate layouts on the rest of the copies of your quilt. You can stick with the same four doodles by simply changing where you put them or the ways you draw them, or you can pick four new doodle designs to work with. Compare your plans. Which do you like best? It's always a good practice to draft out your quilt (or a section of it) before you start quilting. Even experienced free-motion quilters do this to test out their ideas. Mapping out your design will help you feel calmer when you start to quilt.

DAY 24: FLOWERS

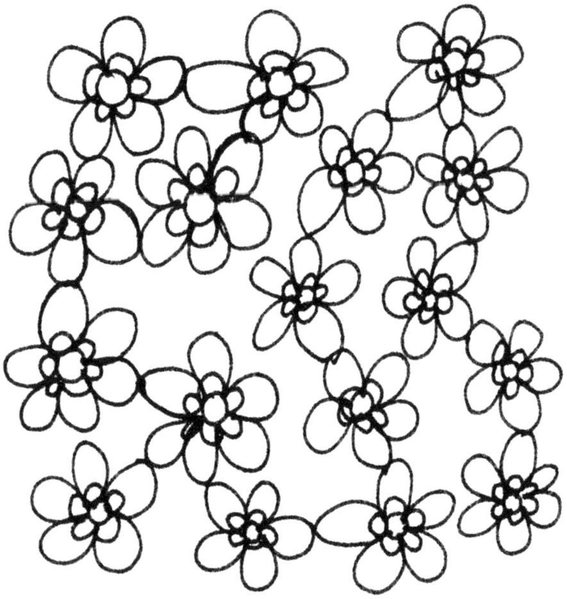

Prompt

Flowers take all kinds of shapes and sizes. Some have petals that curve around a center; others are bell-shape. Some have dozens of petals; others have only three. Flowers also grow in many ways. Some grow on bushes while others grow on vines. Some have a single stem while others branch out from many stems. There are blossoms that grow along branches of trees and water lilies, which float on water.

There is so much variety among flowers! We could probably doodle only flowers for 31 days and never run out of new ideas.

Technical Assistance

When you're drawing flowers with petals radiating from a center, do you have trouble making your petals similar in size and evenly spaced? That's a common problem.

Fortunately, it's easy to fix with a few small guiding marks.

First, draw a flower center within a larger circle. Think about how big you want the center to be in comparison to the petals. The petals fit between the 2 circles.

Next, think about how many petals you want and make marks around the center circle to divide the space equally. If you want 5 petals, make 5 marks in the areas where you would see the points of a five-pointed star. If you want 6 petals, draw 2 marks directly across from each other and then divide the spaces between the 2 marks into 3 spaces using 2 marks between each of the original marks. If you want more petals, subdivide these areas.

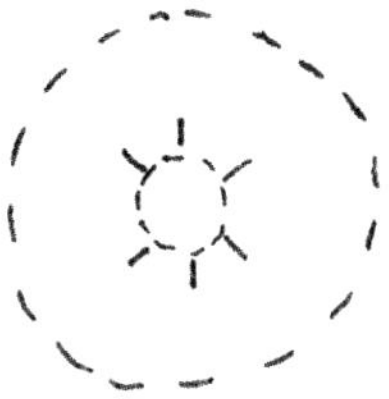

Then, trace around the center circle as if you were stitching it. Draw the first petal between 2 of the marks, extending it to the larger circle. If you are drawing lots of petals around a small center, you might want to keep your petals slender. If you aren't drawing very many petals or your center is large, you can make the petals fatter. If you are trying to create a specific flower, use a photo of that flower as your guide when you create the petal shape.

Continue traveling around the center circle and drawing petals between the marks. When you're finished, the petals should be evenly spaced and roughly the same width and length. Travel along a petal to get to the outside edge of the flower. Practice drawing flowers using guidelines for a while. Eventually, you will be able to draw more even and balanced flowers without having to draw any guidelines.

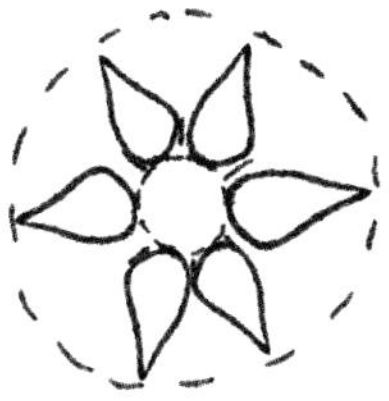

Applications

1 **ASYMMETRICAL ECHOED FLOWER:** This a simple design that fills up an entire quilt block in a hurry. Draw a box on your paper to represent a quilt block. Doodle a simple radiating flower. Place the flower off-center within the block.

Then, simply echo the flower until it fills the block. When you reach the border of the block, travel along the border a bit and then echo the flower in the opposite direction. You may end up with a small area of your flower that is cut off from the main area. To echo that section, travel along the border to that area, echo back and forth until the area is full, then use the border to travel back out.

2 **STAR FLOWER:** Doodle this flower with a small center. If you need guidelines, draw 5 lines that radiate out from a center point, as they would on a star.

Then, draw 5 teardrop-shape petals between these marks. Make your petals fairly large and long.

Next, echo inside each petal with a teardrop-shape. Then, echo around the outside of each petal with a larger petal that has a pointed tip. Finished!

3 SIMPLE ROSE DESIGN: Start out as if you were creating a swirl. Spiral into the center and begin to curve back out. Instead of simply echoing the spiral, draw a series of scallops around the spiral to indicate the first row of rose petals.

Next, reverse the direction you are traveling and echo the first layer of scallops with another layer. Try not to echo the first layer of petals precisely. Stagger the scallops a bit to create a full, overlapping rose petal effect. You can make the rose bigger with more layers or end with two.

Coaching

Deciding on the Thread Color and Why

Let's look ahead to when you start actually quilting your doodles. Let's talk about thread color. If you are a beginning quilter, we recommend that you use a contrasting thread color when practicing quilting. With a contrasting thread, you can see where you need to improve. Write on your practice pieces. Circle some of the problem spots and take notes.

When it comes time for you to quilt a real quilt, we recommend that you use matching thread until you become quite skilled. When you quilt with a matching thread, your thread blends in with your fabric and fades into the shadows. The mistakes you make in your quilting are less obvious so you're less likely to get discouraged when you make mistakes.

Another benefit of matching your thread to the quilt fabric is that the beautiful patterns and piecing in the quilt top don't get hidden by loud quilting. Save your bright, beautiful novelty threads for when you have a little more experience and when your quilts will benefit from a little extra punch.

DAY 25: ARROWS

Prompt

Have you ever thought of arrows as a free-motion quilting design? They are much more adaptable than you might think. For one thing, they don't all need to be straight. Think about a motel's curved *Vacancy* arrow and you'll get what we mean. Arrows can be short and fat or short and thin. They can be long and loopy or long and hooked.

Lately, arrows are a popular symbol in Bohemian fashion. You'll often see arrows decked out with flowers, feathers, or any number of things. Search "boho arrow" online to see some examples.

Technical Assistance

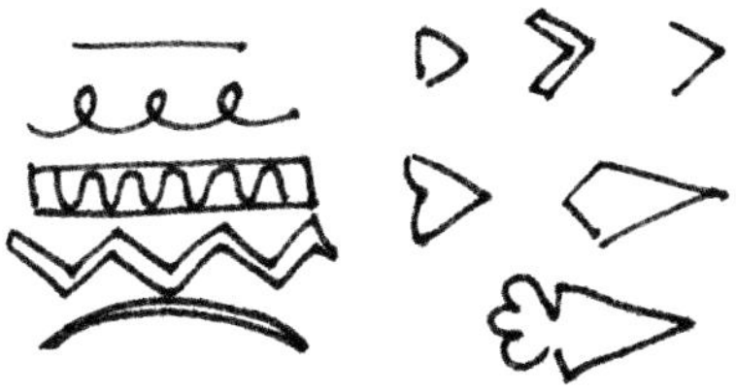

The things to consider when you're doodling or quilting an arrow are the size and shape of the shaft and the size and shape of the head. So, do you want your shaft to be thick, thin, or somewhere in between? Do you want it to be straight, bent, loopy, zigzagged, or something else? Do you want the head to be triangle-shape, diamond-shape like a Native American arrowhead, or maybe just a pointy angle?

Also think of some things that you could use to embellish an arrow. You might want to put feathers at the end or blinking lights around the outside. Perhaps you could make it boho and attach a flower to the shaft. Or maybe you could make road signs with your arrows by putting them in squares and writing *ONE WAY* above them.

Think of as many iterations as you can. Draw every combination you can think of and then figure out how you can doodle your favorite combinations using a continuous line. Next, think about how you could connect your arrows to create a free-motion fill. How could you use your arrows in a border? How could you continuous-line doodle them in geometric shapes? We're excited to see what you come up with.

Applications

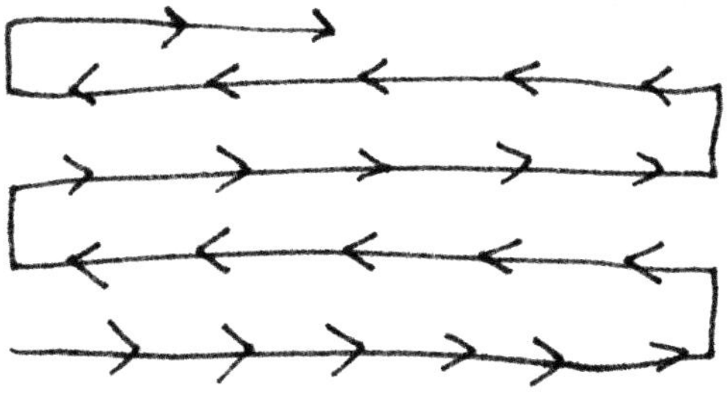

1 **BACK-AND-FORTH ARROWS:** You might want your ruler for this one. Draw a box on your paper. Start drawing a horizontal line near the bottom left of the box. Draw triangle or pointy shapes at regular intervals as you form the line. When you reach the border, travel up and draw another line of arrows from right to left. Face the arrow points the opposite direction from the arrows above and stagger them so that they aren't directly over the points below. Continue in this manner, alternating directions and staggering the points in each row, until the box is full. You can also draw this design using diagonal or vertical arrow shaft lines.

2 EVERY-WHICH-WAY ARROWS: This design is a great way to quilt out a square space. Draw a square on your paper to start. Starting from any edge of the square, draw an arrow pointing into the inside of the square. Draw the arrow using a continuous line, drawing one side of the shaft first, then the point, and then the other side, ending back at the edge of the square. Make the point and the shaft fairly thick.

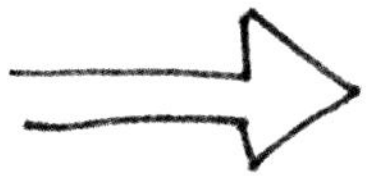

Travel along the edge of the square to another area and draw another arrow pointing into the square. Continue drawing arrows until you are satisfied with your design or your square is full.

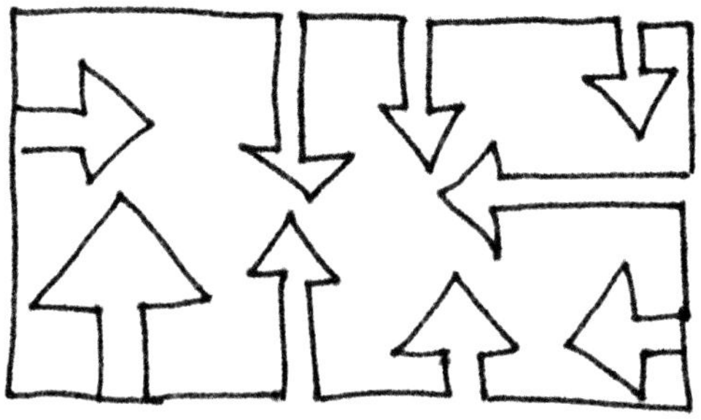

---

3 LOOPY LOVE ARROWS: This design looks great in quilt sashing. It's nice and narrow. Start by forming two horizontal guidelines across your paper. Between your two guidelines, on the left side of your paper, draw the feathery-looking tail of an arrow. Draw a short, straight line from the tail. Form the lowercase word *love* in a continuous line, the same way you would write it in cursive. Draw another short line coming out of the end of the **E** and then draw a pointy tip. Meander along your sashing with a loopy line. Form more arrows along the line at intervals.

Coaching

Scale Consideration

It may have occurred to you that the scale of your doodles needs to be rather small to fit onto your page. When you're quilting your quilts, however, you are usually filling larger spaces and you'll need to increase the scale of your free-motion designs. It's a good idea to doodle them out in their final scale before you quilt them.

Remember the clear vinyl trick we told you about in Day 15: Crisscross (see Vinyl Over Top of Quilt, page 61)? That's the quickest and easiest way to doodle your design at full size. If you don't have vinyl, draft out a block or a section of your quilt and doodle your design to-scale there.

When you get a little more experience, changing the scale of your designs becomes natural. For your first few quilts, however, we suggest that you doodle at least one block to scale. This will provide more peace of mind about taking your doodles to your quilt.

DAY 26: SHELLS

Prompt

Isn't nature wonderful? Our earth creates its own ornaments in so many ways. Take shells, for example. They're like lace or jewelry that the ocean makes. Shells are often beautifully fluted and ridged; some have gorgeous spotted patterns or stripes or they are shimmery and opalescent inside. They can be lovely shapes, such as spirals, cones, half-circles, and more.

Many quilters favor clamshells. However, there are also great shells in various other shapes and sizes, such as conch shells, cowrie shells, keyhole limpets, sand dollars, and starfish shells.

Technical Assistance

To get started, let's make a simple snail shell. Start by spiraling in, as if you were drawing a swirl. Then, draw a C-curve that echoes the center of the spiral.

Continue drawing C-curves as you work your way around the inside of the spiral, toward the opening. Make the C-curves with a back-and-forth motion, merging the ends of the curves with the outline of the spiral. You can also travel along the spiral outline a bit to keep the curves evenly spaced.

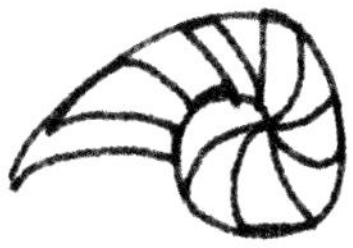

This could also be the beginning of a live snail. Can you imagine how you would add a body, head, and antenna?

Applications

1 **OCEAN SNAIL SHELL VARIATION:** Start by spiraling into a swirl. Spiral out, closely echoing the inside C-cup of the spiral. Spiral all the way around the outside of the swirl and merge the end of the line with the starting line.

Draw a scallop shape on the inside of the swirl (as shown).

Use matchstick lines, back and forth, to shade the inside of the scallop shape. Trace counterclockwise along the outside of the swirl for a bit and draw a scallop shape that attaches to the right side of the swirl.

Reverse directions and travel back along the scallop a bit, then draw a smaller scallop shape attached to the right of the first. Continue this until the final scallop shape is quite small and the swirl shell has taken on a cone shape.

2 OYSTER FILL: Draw a 6″ square. Starting at a border, draw a small oyster shell–shape inside the square that starts and finishes at the same point. To make the shape "oystery," instead of like a paisley or a clam, make it elongated with a slightly flattened curved end (as shown). Echo the first oyster shape with a line that diverges gradually from the start point and then merges back with the start point at its end.

Echo the oyster shape as many times as you like. You can draw another oyster from the same starting point as the first oyster or travel around the outside edge of the first oyster and start a second oyster in another area. Repeat this design to fill the space you have available.

---

3 SIMPLE STARFISH: Draw a small circle as the center of the starfish. Imagine you are drawing a flower with 5 skinny, pointed petals. Draw 5 large petal shapes radiating out from the circle.

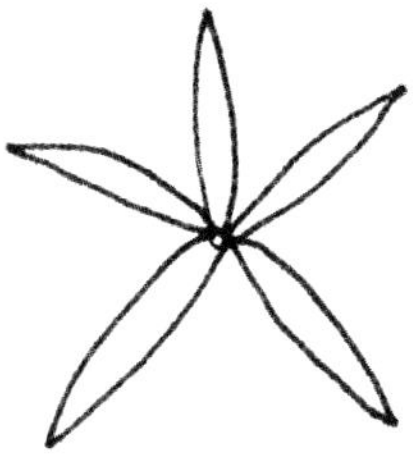

Travel out to the tip of one of the petals. Draw a line that diverges from the petal tip, dipping slightly toward the center of the starfish. When you near the center between petals, curve the line to echo the space between the 2 petals and then merge the line with the tip of the adjacent petal. Repeat between the next 2 petals, and all around the starfish until you arrive back at the petal where you started.

4 **SAND DOLLAR:** Draw a small circle with 5 thin petal shapes radiating out from it. Make these petals shorter than you did for the starfish. Travel to the outer tip of 1 petal shape and draw a circle around and enclose the star flower–shape. This circle can be a bit wavy and uneven.

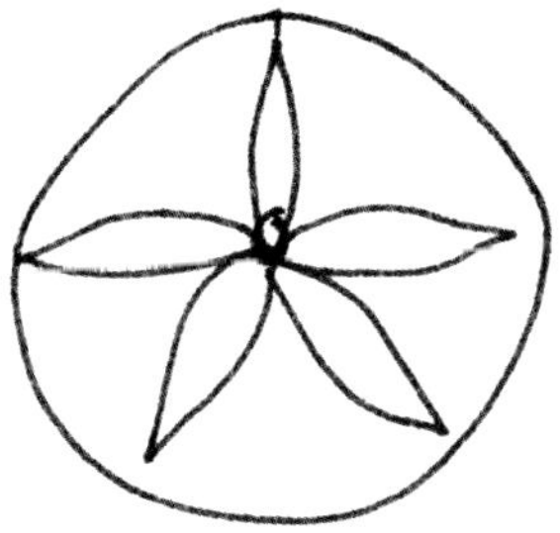

Coaching

Doodle to Domestic

This coaching is for those of you who will be free-motion quilting on a domestic machine. If you plan to quilt on a longarm you can skip this coaching section and begin Day 27: Windows (next page).

If you need help setting up your machine, making a quilt sandwich, or any other aspect of free-motion quilting on your domestic machine, we recommend Dara's book *Walk, Jog, Run—A Free-Motion Quilting Workout* (page 126).

Here are our best tips for getting started:

- When you doodle, you use one hand to guide your pen around the paper. When you free-motion quilt on a domestic machine, you move your quilt under the needle. You'll find, however, that your brain quickly makes the switch. Your mind translates the motion and the traveling path you learned through your doodles as you quilt.
- Focus on one design at a time. Quilt it until you feel confident and like your results. Then choose another design and get really good at that design. Once you have confidence in two designs, blend them together.
- Don't worry at first about keeping your stitch length consistent. Consistent stitch length often comes naturally, over time. We don't want you to have to think about too many things at once.

DAY 27: WINDOWS

Prompt

We can probably guess what you are thinking.... Window? This is a strange prompt.

Think about the purpose of a window. It lets the light in. It keeps the light out. It allows new views. It lets the breeze pass through. It casts shadows....

Think about the variety of windows. There are endless sizes, shapes, and configurations. How does the purpose of a window affect its size and shape and even its color? Think of all of this. Now take the first thought or picture in your head and start to doodle.

Technical Assistance

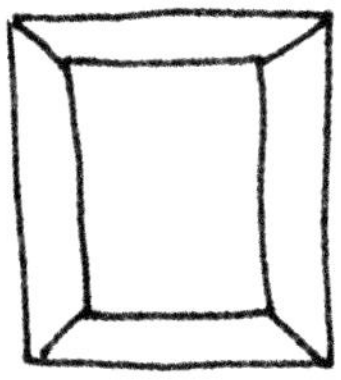

How would you form a basic rectangular window that has multiple panes? Start with the outside shape. If you would like casing around the window, use a diagonal line in the corner to travel inside the rectangle, and then echo the window on the inside, drawing a diagonal line into each corner to make the casing look mitered.

To create pane segments inside of the window, draw 2 or 3 lines vertically (traveling along the border between the lines). Then add 2 or 3 lines horizontally, again traveling along the border between the lines in the same manner.

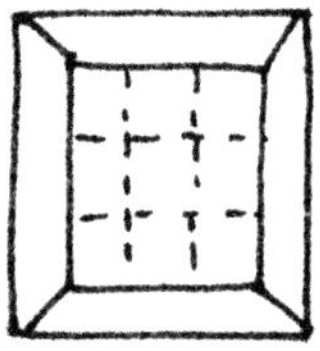

Alternatively, if you'd like a little space between the panes, that's also easy to accomplish. Before you begin, mark some light guidelines. Lightly draw the basic window shape—in this case a large rectangle—then draw in a light grid. As you start to doodle this window, begin with the outside lines. Then, if you want to add a casing follow the instructions for the basic window. After you doodle the casing, use a short line to travel into the nearest square of the grid. Closely echo the shape of the square to create the first pane.

Travel along the first pane and use a short line to get into the next square of the grid. Echo that square in the same manner. Repeat these steps to create all the panes.

Applications

1 **CURTAINED WINDOWS:** This design works well in a series of windows that are next to each other. Lightly draw 3 tall rectangles in a row for guidelines. Beginning at the bottom left corner of the first rectangle, or window, on the left, draw around the entire outline of the window. Next, draw a long scallop shape inside the rectangle. It should reach from the bottom left corner to the top left corner of the window. Echo the inside of the scallop twice to give it a drape-like look. Finish in the top left corner of the window.

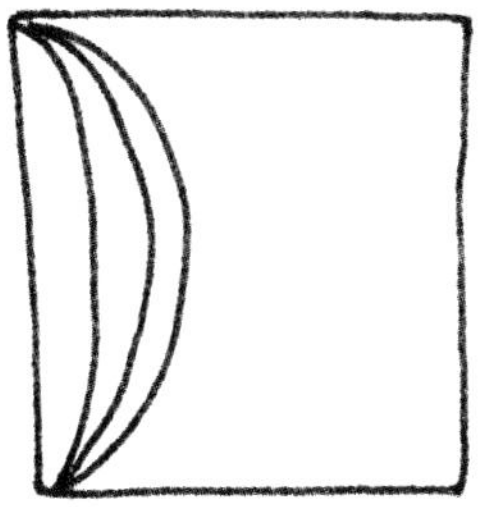

Draw another, shorter scallop from the top left to the top right corner of the window. Echo the scallop twice and end in the top right corner.

Draw a third scallop from the top right corner to the bottom right corner and echo it twice, ending in the bottom right corner.

Travel from the base of the first window to the bottom left corner of the second window. Repeat the steps you followed for the first window to create the second and third windows.

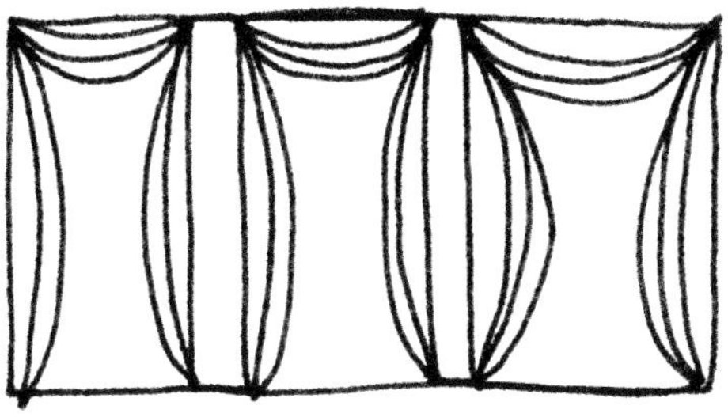

---

2 **ROCK HOUSE WINDOW:** Let's take a stone wall and throw in a window. Go back to Day 20: Walls, application 2. Stone Wall (page 81), if you need to review. Draw a 6″ square on your paper. Draw 2 rows of stones along the bottom inside of the square. In the third row, put the base of the window into the middle of the row. Make the window base stones larger and squarer than the rest of the stones in the row. When you finish the window base, create the rest of the window by forming a square of these square-shape stones in a smaller size.

Fill in the stone wall to the left of the window. Travel across the top and down the right side of the window, creating stones in the wall as you travel. Fill in the area to the right of your window with stones. Make another row or two of stones above your window to finish.

Coaching

Doodle to Longarm

We did some coaching for domestic machine quilters in Day 26: Shells (page 104). Today's coaching is for longarm quilters. If you plan to quilt on a domestic machine, skip ahead to the beginning of Day 28: Rainbows (next page).

If you need help setting up your machine or any other aspect of free-motion quilting on your longarm, we recommend Dara's book *Walk, Jog, Run—A Free-Motion Quilting Workout* (page 126).

Here are our best tips for getting started:

- When you doodle, you use one hand to guide your pen around the paper. When you free-motion quilt on a longarm, you move the sew head with both hands to move the needle and create your design. You'll find, however, that your brain easily makes the switch. Your mind translates the motion and the traveling path you learned through your doodles as you quilt.
- Focus on one design at a time. Quilt it until you feel confident. Then choose another design and get really good at that design. Once you have confidence in two designs, blend them together.
- Your longarm may have stitch regulation but if not, don't worry about keeping your stitch length consistent. Focus on moving the machine with a smooth steady motion to create your design. Consistent stitch length often comes naturally over time.

DAY 28: RAINBOWS

Prompt

This would be a great prompt for introducing color to your doodles, if you haven't already. After all, what's a rainbow without colors?

What do we associate with rainbows, in addition to their brilliant colors? What about rain and rain clouds—you can't have rain or rainbows without them. Along with rain and clouds, what about birds or kites or airplanes? Don't forget about big pots of gold!

Technical Assistance

One challenge with doodling rainbows is keeping the arches consistently spaced. Have you been remembering to practice glancing ahead to where you're headed while you quilt?

A tip is to keep the doodles on a smaller scale. On a small scale, it's easy to see if the curves follow each other. When your scale gets large, your lines tend to drift off after you go over the top of the curve.

If you have a curved ruler in your house, that can also help. You might need to reposition it around the arch as the rainbow grows but it will still help you keep your lines steady.

If you don't have a ruler, try creating a series of templates out of a cereal box or other thin cardboard. Creating templates is a bit of work, we admit it. A bonus to doing this, however, is that you can reuse your templates over and over again. You can even make another set and use them to mark your quilt tops if you don't have rulers that will do the job. Make them like the examples on the right.

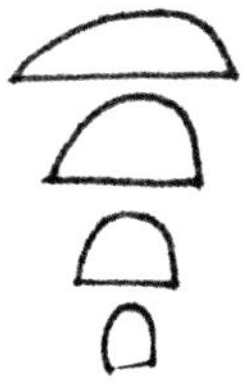

Applications

1 **MIXED-UP RAINBOWS AND CLOUDS:** This design makes your rainbows look like they're weaving in and out and around each other. Start by drawing your favorite continuous-line cloud. Draw the first line of a rainbow arching out from the cloud. At the end of this line draw another cloud.

After you finish the second cloud, travel along the outside of the cloud to where you need to branch off to complete the first band of the rainbow. Echo the first arch, then travel along the first cloud a bit and echo the second arch. Continue until you have as many bands as you want.

Then, draw a line arcing out from anywhere within the design. At the end, draw another cloud. Complete the rainbow arch by echoing it back to where you started and traveling along that line a bit and then echoing back and forth, as you did for the first rainbow.

Repeat the steps above to create more rainbows and clouds. If you need to travel to another area, use previous lines you've made. Try to fill the space evenly, but don't worry if you have some small gaps with nothing in them. That's just sky.

2 RAINBOW VARIETY PACK: This time, start by drawing 1 big rainbow. (Temporarily forget what we told you about keeping the scale small.) Starting in whichever band is closest to your pen, fill a band with a design that you can string along inside it. You could put pebbles, swirls, zigzags, loops, Greek keys, daisy chains, leafy vines, strings of stars, or anything else that will fit into the band. When you've filled up the first band, travel along the base of the rainbow to the next band and fill it with a different design. Continue until you've filled the entire rainbow.

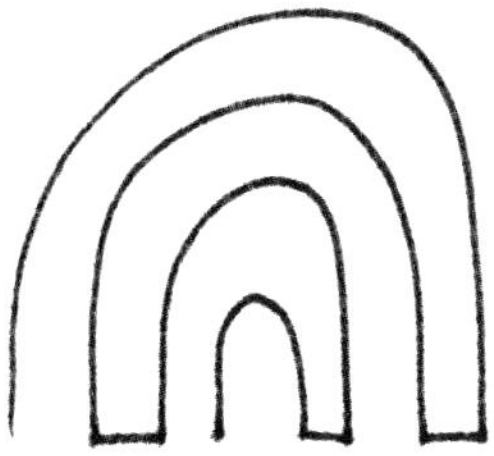

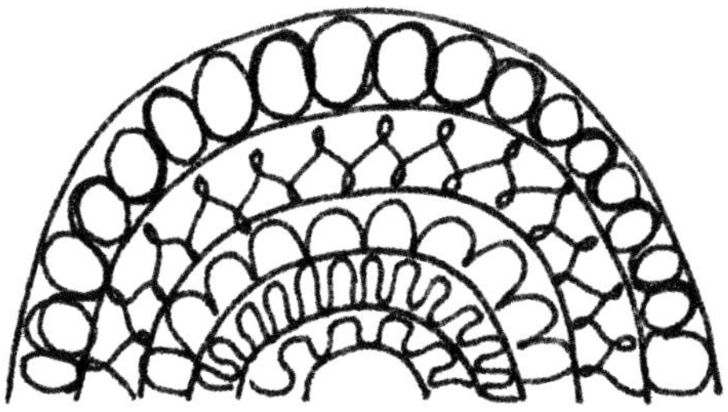

---

3 RAINBOW BORDER DESIGN: If you made cardboard templates, you'll want to use them for this one. Draw 2 solid lines across your paper to represent the border, spacing the lines so that you can fit the tallest template between them. If you don't have templates, space them 3″ apart.

If you didn't make templates, we suggest you make marks to indicate the beginning and end of each rainbow along the border. Make each rainbow the same size across. The top line of the border indicates where the arches of the rainbows should peak. You can make marks along the top of the border to indicate these points.

Draw the top of the first arch inside the border guidelines. Travel along the bottom line of the border a little bit inside the first arch. Draw an arch that's slightly shorter and echoes inside the first arch.

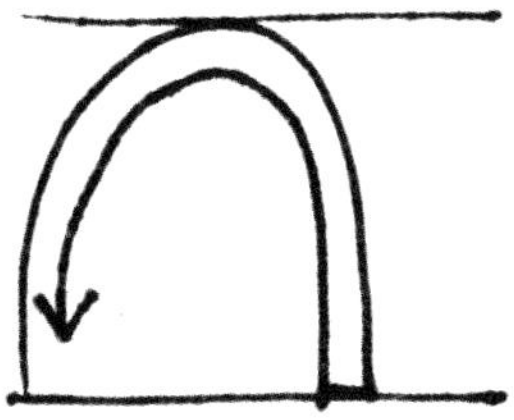

Repeat this for each ribbon of the rainbow, reversing the direction you're traveling each time. If you're lucky, you'll end on the right side and it will be a short distance to travel to the outside of the rainbow and begin your next one.

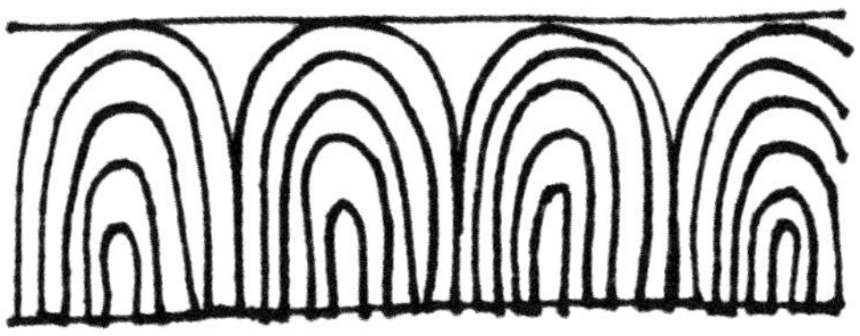

Coaching

Doodle to Domestic Machine

If you've practiced one design until you're comfortable with it, you are probably ready to master a second design. Once you feel good about creating your second design, we recommend you practice blending the two designs together. If you start blending designs early you will be able to do it with any new design that you learn.

Try combining the two designs you've learned best to create a background fill. Nest clusters of them together. Throw in some echoing to make traveling easier and to fill up some of the small spaces. We've doodled a background fill that combines swirls and clouds as an example.

DAY 29: ZIGZAGS

Prompt

Have you noticed how much energy there is in a zigzag pattern? A straight line feels perfectly still. Put that straight line into a back and forth zigzag pattern, and it instantly becomes full of movement and expression.

Zigzags can feel angry, excited, or bold. They can feel charged with energy and electricity. A zigzag design in your quilting never fails to liven it up.

Technical Assistance

When you put rows of zigzags next to each other—echoing each other—they become chevrons. Chevrons allow you to continue practicing your even spacing skills. If you don't want to wing it, pull out that ruler again.

A key to making beautiful chevrons is making sure their points stay lined up, like soldiers in a row. That's the structure that keeps those zigging and zagging lines from getting out of control.

Draw a 6″ square. Make a row of evenly spaced zigzags along the bottom of the square, traveling left to right. Next, use a ruler to make dots that are evenly spaced above each zig (peak) of the first row of zigzags.

From the end of the first row, travel up the right border of the square. Traveling right to left, connect the first row of dots that you made above the peaks and valleys to form the second row. Travel up the left border of the square and repeat, traveling back and forth across the paper until you have filled in your square with the chevron pattern.

Applications

1 **TRAVELING ZIGZAGS BORDER DESIGN:** Draw 2 parallel guidelines across your paper, 2″ apart, to represent a border. Draw marks every 2″ along the top line. On the bottom line, make a mark that is staggered over 1″ from the left edge. From the 1″ mark, make marks every 2″ along the bottom line. Connect the marks with a zigzag line, from left to right. Your line travels from the first mark on the top line to the 1″ mark on the bottom line and then continues back and forth.

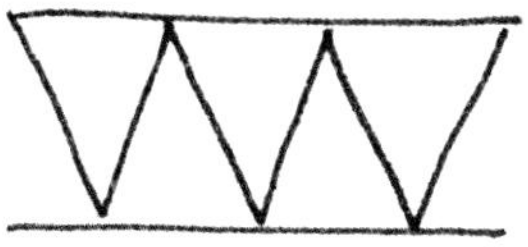

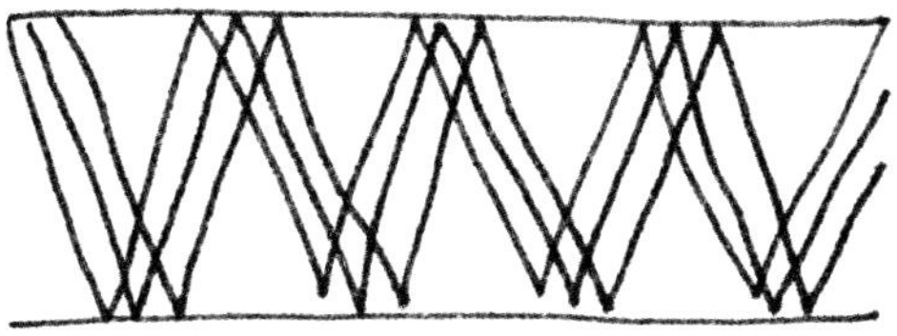

Travel ⅛″ along the top guideline. Draw another zigzag that echoes the first one ⅛″ to the left. The bottom of the last zigzag echo is cut off if it extends off the paper. That's okay. Travel up the edge of the paper ⅛″, if you need to, or travel along the bottom line ⅛″ to the left of the echo to create a second zigzag line that echoes the last one on the left. Repeat, traveling back and forth across the border as many times as you like.

If you draw so many echoes that the lines meet up with the first zigzags, you will have created a diamond grid and your zigzag pattern will disappear.

2 **MOUNTAIN PEAKS:** You've doodled chevrons. Now, let's make some truly irregular zigzags. Draw a square on the paper to represent a quilt block. Draw a row of zigzags above the bottom of the block. Make these zigzags look jagged. Make some of the angles very sharp, and some of them wide.

Travel up the margin of the square and draw another row of zigzags above the first. Again, make these zigzags look jagged. You can echo the first row, but sometimes do it in a very loose, slanted way—don't make your echoes exactly parallel. Repeat these types of rows, traveling back and forth across the block. Stop before the peaks hit the top of the block if you want a little sky above your mountains.

3 **STATIC CHARGED FEATHER:** We imagine this is what traditional free-motion feathers would look like if you rubbed them on your hair. Start by drawing a square to represent a quilt block. Draw a wavy spine from one corner of the block to the opposite corner. Echo the spine, merging the echo with the other side of the spine at the tips.

Travel back a bit along the echo line. Draw a lightning bolt-style zigzag from the spine to the nearest border of the block. Echo the lightning bolt back to the spine.

Travel a little farther along the spine and draw another lightning bolt that reaches across the block diagonally and echoes back to the spine. Repeat until you have filled up the space on this side of the spine with lightning bolts. Travel to the other side of the spine and fill that side up with lightning bolts that travel along the spine and reach across to the opposite edge of the block.

Coaching

Do Your Research

Planning out a design for a quilt is so much easier than it once was. If you have quilting books to browse through, that's great! If you don't, a simple search on the internet will bring up dozens of ideas for you to play with. If the quilt you are working on is a common quilt pattern, or contains traditional quilt blocks, just search the name of the quilt or the blocks. If your quilt has a theme, such as a beach quilt, try searching something like "beach quilting designs." You can also search on Pinterest. We've found that a search on an internet browser and a Pinterest search tend to bring up different results.

DAY 30: BORDERS

Prompt

When you think about borders, our guess is that the first thing you picture is borders on a quilt. So, for today's prompt, why not learn some new border designs?

You can also stretch yourself a bit further and create designs based on other definitions of the word *border*. For example, think about a garden border. What would that look like if you drew it with a continuous line? You can also think about the word as a verb—*to border* is basically to be close or next to something else. Like how Nevada borders California by being next to it and running alongside it.

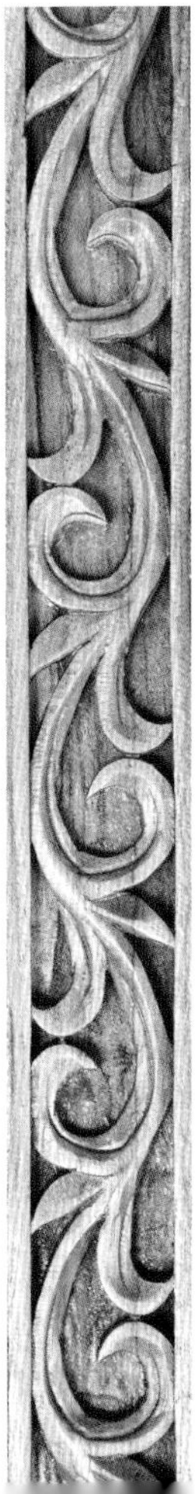

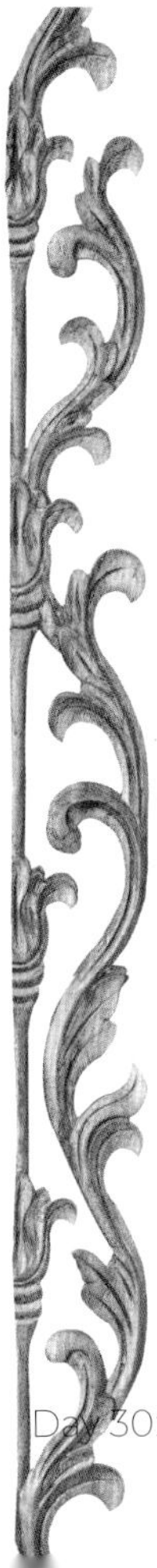

Technical Assistance

For many free-motion border designs, as with so much of free-motion quilting, even spacing is key. Use your seams to keep your design a consistent height or width.

Your design can either touch your seams, or you can draw or imagine guidelines within your seams to keep your design from touching them.

When you are trying to fill the border of a quilt with a repeat design, it's important to divide it into even lengthwise sections. Get into that habit by evenly marking the spaces in doodle borders. Measure the entire length and then divide the length by the number of repeats you want to put into it.

You can divide your quilt borders more easily if you have a roll of adding machine tape. Stretch a piece of adding machine tape across the quilt border and cut it to the same length. Fold the tape in half at the center, fold the halved tape in half at the center, and so on, until you have folded it into the size of sections you want. Unfold the tape and use it to mark your border.

Applications

1 **HEARTS AND LOOPS:** Draw 2 guidelines to represent a narrow border on the paper. Using the bottom line as the base, draw a small loop with its base against the bottom line and its loop pointed toward the top line.

Coming out of the loop, draw a curve to form a larger loop. At the top of the large loop, flatten the curve and draw a small loop inside the large loop the points back toward the base.

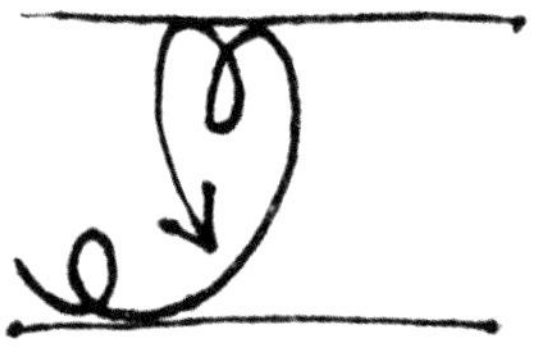

Come out of this small loop with a hooked curve that mirrors the other side of the large loop and finishes the large loop near your baseline. Can you see how the larger loop became a heart when you put a small loop at the top?

Continue across the border, alternating between small loops and hearts.

2 **SPIRAL VINE:** Draw guidelines 2″ apart on the paper to represent a border. Draw a spiral traveling from left to right inside the border guidelines. Your spiral can touch a border, or even both borders, if you want.

Travel out of the spiral until you are somewhere on the right side of its outside curve. Start a second spiral. This time, spiral in the opposite direction. If you curved toward the bottom guideline when you started the first spiral, curve the second spiral toward the top guideline.

Travel along the border, creating spirals that alternate directions. When you feel comfortable with the motion, throw in random smaller spirals that branch out from the larger spirals.

3 **SPIRAL FLOWER GARDEN BORDER:** This is a design that Amy created. It takes 3 passes to complete the design. Draw 1½″ border guidelines horizontally across the paper. Divide the border into thirds by drawing 2 dotted horizontal lines evenly spaced between them.

Working from left to right, draw a series of arches, starting and ending with a half-arch. Make the arches as tall as the lower dotted line.

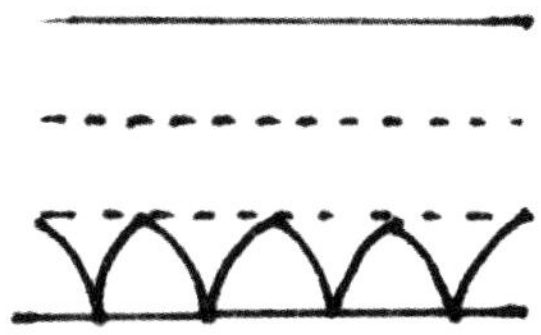

Reverse direction and draw a series of upside-down arches. The curves of the arches should meet up with the bases of the arches from the first pass. Where the upside-down curves meet up with the bases, draw short, vertical lines. These lines become the stems of the flowers.

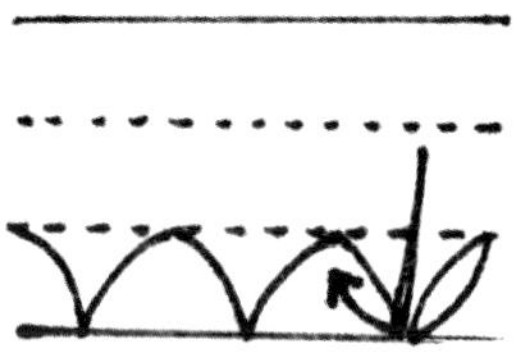

When you reach the left side of the border, travel up the edge a bit. Then, draw a spiral directly on top of the first stem to the right. Start at the center of the spiral and spiral out from the center until the flower is the size you want. Swoop over to the top of the next stem and repeat. Draw spiral flowers on all the stems along the border.

Coaching

Execute the Design

Coming up with a quilting plan for an entire quilt doesn't need to be complicated.

Have you noticed how one design can change significantly if you fit it into a new shape or quilt it in a new way? If you've mastered pebbles, for example, try fitting a string of pebbles inside a triangle and then inside sashing.

You can quilt an entire quilt with only one or two basic designs and still make the quilting interesting and varied.

DAY 31: SPIDER WEBS

Prompt

Our final prompt is a favorite among doodlers and quilters alike—the spider web.

Spider web designs are the go-to for any Halloween quilt. You can put them into corners or fill a whole quilt with them. While you're at it, learn some spider designs. Place a few in your webs or dangling from them and the design instantly gets creepier.

Have you thought about using spider webs on nature-themed quilts? You can easily work them into panels, maybe strung across branches of trees or blades of grass. Have you noticed that old-fashioned crazy quilts nearly always have a spider web and a spider on them somewhere? It was for good luck. What would you think about hiding a web and a spider in some of your quilting, to pass on the tradition?

Technical Assistance

You've probably been drawing spider webs for as long as you can remember. What you most likely haven't been doing is drawing them with continuous lines. By now, however, we know you're a pro at figuring out your travel path and not lifting your pen.

- *For a basic spider web:* First, draw a big asterisk shape, traveling out each leg and back into the center. Next, draw swooping scallops, starting at the center of the asterisk. Travel with inverted scallop shapes from 1 leg of the frame to the next, around in a spiral. Stop when you decide it looks right.

- *To fill an entire area with webs:* Draw a line branching out from the first web and repeat the process. If your webs start to run into each other, travel along the outside line of any web you run into to reach another area and start another web. Of course, since these are spider webs, they can also crisscross over each other and look messy and wispy. It's up to you.

Applications

1 **SPIDER WEB BORDER:** This border design creates the illusion of a web, even without the framework in the center. Draw border guidelines on the paper, about 3″ apart. Start on the left side of the border and at the center of the first web, draw small inverted scallop shapes that start to spiral out and around each other.

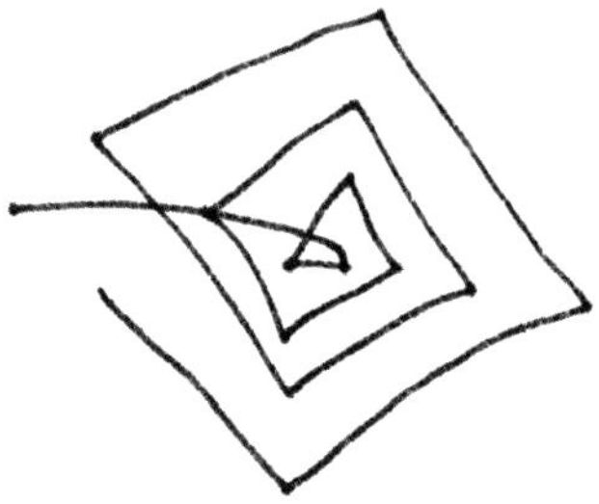

Continue spiraling around with inverted scallops. As you travel around, try to line up the points of the inverted scallops. You'll need to make them bigger as you spiral out in order to keep the points lined up. When your web fits nicely into your border. Use a swooping, curved line to travel to the center of the next web and repeat. Continue building webs all along your border.

2 **FAT SPIDER:** Draw a line straight down from any line of a spider web. At the end of the line, draw a big circle. Traveling around the circle, create legs by drawing inverted V-shapes, out from and then back to the circle. Put 4 legs on the right of the circle and 4 on the left. To make your spider look black, fill in the inside of the circle with matchstick lines.

---

3 **CURLY WEBS:** This web is just the basic web with some curls attached but somehow the curls make it so cute! You know how to draw a basic web. Draw a framework and start to form a scalloped spiral around it. When you draw your scallops, pause part way through some of them and draw a little C-curve or a small spiral branching out in any direction from the curve.

Coaching

Share and Celebrate

You've made it! We hope you are proud of yourself. What you've accomplished is no small thing. You've proven to yourself that you can decide to do something and then stick with it to the end.

We have some final requests. First, celebrate this accomplishment. This is a perfect opportunity to show yourself some love.

Next? Share your accomplishments! We hope you've been posting your daily doodles on social media and using our hashtag **#freemotiondoodleschool**. If not, what are you waiting for? We want to give you virtual hugs and celebrate with you. Share your doodles with your family and friends in real time, too. They'll be amazed at what you've learned.

In addition, think about sharing your work at quilt conventions and exhibits. Quilting has a beautiful history and tradition. When you participate in local shows, you help keep the tradition alive and vital. Conventions are also a chance to play, meet new friends, and share your passion.

Finally, keep going. We believe you will continue to do amazing things. You're going to reap big rewards from your consistent, small actions. Keep going with your doodling and your free-motion quilting.

We hope this is only the beginning of your quilting adventures. We encourage you to continue and make the doodle sampler, *Doodles Gone Wild* (page 124). Can you think of a better way to remember and honor your accomplishment? It will become a physical reminder that you are willing to do hard things to accomplish your goals.

DOODLES Gone Wild

Finished quilt:
60½″ × 60½″

Designed, pieced, and quilted by Dara Tomasson

FABRIC REQUIREMENTS

Quilt blocks: 6 assorted solid color fabrics, ¾ yard *each* (I used black, navy, light blue, yellow, green, and red.)

Border: ⅞ yard (I used same light blue as in quilt blocks.)

Backing: 4 yards

Binding: ½ yard

Batting: 68″ × 68″

CUTTING

Assorted solid fabrics

From each color, cut 2 strips 8″ × WOF; subcut into 8″ squares. You will need the following number of squares:

Black: 7 squares

Navy: 7 squares

Light blue: 9 squares

Yellow: 9 squares

Green: 9 squares

Red: 8 squares

Border

Cut 6 strips 4½″ × WOF.

Binding

Cut 7 strips 2¼″ × WOF.

Construction

Seam allowances are ¼″.

1 Arrange 49 squares into 1 panel of 7 × 7 squares. (For color placement, see the completed quilt photo.) Sew the squares together into rows.

Press the seam allowances in all odd-numbered rows (rows 1, 3, 5, and 7) to the right.

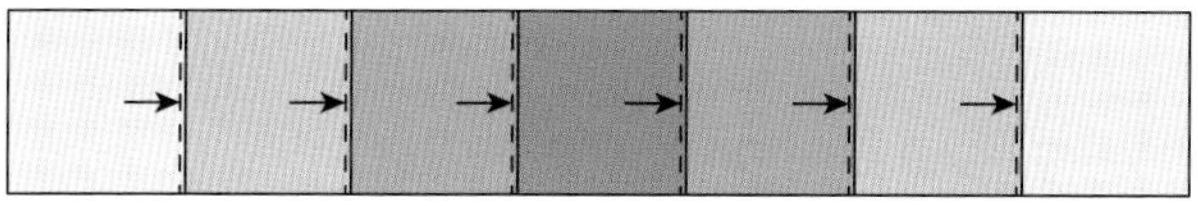

Press the seam allowances in all even-numbered rows (rows 2, 4, and 6) to the left.

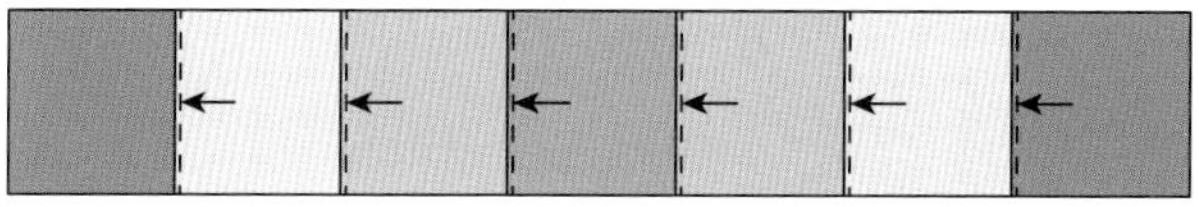

2 Sew the rows together and press the seam allowances in one direction to complete the quilt center.

3 Sew the 4½″ border strips together into one length and press the seams open. From the length, cut 2 strips 53″ long and 2 strips 61″ long.

4 Sew the 53″ strips to the sides of the panel, and press the seam allowances away from the center. Sew the 61″ strips to the top and bottom of the panel, and press the seam allowances away from the center.

5 Piece the backing fabric together as needed to make a 68″ × 68″ panel.

6 If you plan to quilt using your domestic sewing machine, pin or spray baste the backing, batting, and quilt top to make a quilt sandwich, and baste the layers together. If you plan on using a longarm machine, load the top, backing, and batting onto your frame.

7 Quilt as desired in each quilt block. Our border features a variety of feathers, but you can choose your favorite doodle for the border.

8 Join the binding strips end to end on the bias to create one continuous strip. Bind the quilt with your preferred method.

ABOUT THE AUTHORS

Photo by Vanessa Lust

DARA TOMASSON is a free-motion quilting liberator who helps fellow quilters find their own "free-motion quilting voice." Through her in person workshops, her YouTube channel, and online classes, she uses her professional teaching background to build curriculum that takes quilters from where they are and helps them develop new skills.

You will find Dara spending a lot of her day helping fellow quilters lose weight and create more joy in their lives with her life-coaching skills. Not only will Dara liberate your free-motion quilting skills, but she will also liberate your mind so you are ready to create the things that you truly want.

Dara has lived in many Canadian cities but currently resides on Vancouver Island with her husband and five children. Balancing her creative career and raising kids is the best recipe for success.

Visit Dara online and follow on social media!

WEBSITE: daratomasson.com

FACEBOOK: /dara.bowietomasson

INSTAGRAM: @daratomasson

ALSO BY DARA TOMASSON

Photo by Tim Robertson

AMY COLLEEN ROBERTSON's passion for longarm quilting began in 2017, when her youngest child started school full time and she began teaching and sales at a local quilt shop. Almost immediately, she found herself drawn to the longarm machines. She started her longarm quilting business, Dappled Things Quilting, out of her garage in early 2018. Her work continues to be admired and complimented by customers for its unique style and artistry. She was honored to receive the Instructor's Choice award for her *Spirit of the Plains* quilt in the 2019 Utah Quilt Guild's Quilt Fest.

In other endeavors, she developed her first art quilt pattern, March Hare, which she plans to follow with a series of patterns with a children's classical literature theme. She's exploring how to make the quilting and fiber arts industries more sustainable and eco-friendly. Such projects include working with natural materials to create dyes and inks and raising silkworms for spinning and dyeing silk embroidery floss.

Amy met Dara at the 2019 Utah Quilting and Sewing Marketplace, where Dara was a teacher. Their collaboration on this book is one of many wonderful by-products of that meeting.

Visit Amy online and follow on social media!

WEBSITE: dappledthingsbyamy.com

FACEBOOK: /amyrobertsonfiberartandquilting

INSTAGRAM: @dappledthingsbyamy

Want even more creative content?
Visit us online at ctpub.com
FREE PATTERNS | FREE VIDEO TUTORIALS | TOOLS | GIFTS & MORE!
quilt, snap, share